James Macdonald Oxley

The young Woodsman

Or, Life in the Forests of Canada

James Macdonald Oxley

The young Woodsman
Or, Life in the Forests of Canada

ISBN/EAN: 9783337189259

Printed in Europe, USA, Canada, Australia, Japan

Cover: Foto ©ninafisch / pixelio.de

More available books at **www.hansebooks.com**

THE
YOUNG WOODSMAN

OR

Life in the Forests of Canada

BY

J. MACDONALD OXLEY

*Author of "Diamond Rock; or, On the Right Track,"
&c. &c.*

T. NELSON AND SONS
London, Edinburgh, and New York

1895

CONTENTS.

I. THE CALL TO WORK,	9
II. THE CHOICE OF AN OCCUPATION,	20
III. OFF TO THE WOODS,	32
IV. THE BUILDING OF THE SHANTY,	44
V. STANDING FIRE,	58
VI. LIFE IN THE LUMBER CAMP,	69
VII. A THRILLING EXPERIENCE,	81
VIII. IN THE NICK OF TIME,	94
IX. OUT OF CLOUDS, SUNSHINE,	105
X. A HUNTING-TRIP,	116
XI. THE GREAT SPRING DRIVE,	130
XII. HOME AGAIN,	144

THE YOUNG WOODSMAN.

CHAPTER I.

THE CALL TO WORK.

"I 'M afraid there'll be no more school for you now, Frank darling. Will you mind having to go to work?"

"Mind it! Why, no, mother; not the least bit. I'm quite old enough, ain't I?"

"I suppose you are, dear; though I would like to have you stay at your lessons for one more year anyway. What kind of work would you like best?"

"That's not a hard question to answer, mother. I want to be what father was."

The mother's face grew pale at this reply, and for some few moments she made no response.

*   *   *   *   *

The march of civilization on a great continent

means loss as well as gain. The opening up of the country for settlement, the increase and spread of population, the making of the wilderness to blossom as the rose, compel the gradual retreat and disappearance of interesting features that can never be replaced. The buffalo, the beaver, and the elk have gone; the bear, the Indian, and the forest in which they are both most at home, are fast following.

Along the northern border of settlement in Canada there are flourishing villages and thriving hamlets to-day where but a few years ago the verdurous billows of the primeval forest rolled in unbroken grandeur. The history of any one of these villages is the history of all. An open space beside the bank of a stream or the margin of a lake presented itself to the keen eye of the woodranger traversing the trackless waste of forest as a fine site for a lumber camp. In course of time the lumber camp grew into a depot from which other camps, set still farther back in the depths of the "limits," are supplied. Then the depot develops into a settlement surrounded by farms; the settlement gathers itself into a village with shops, schools, churches, and hotels; and so the process of growth goes on, the forest ever retreating as the dwellings of men multiply.

THE CALL TO WORK.

It was in a village with just such a history, and bearing the name of Calumet, occupying a commanding situation on a vigorous tributary of the Ottawa River—the Grand River, as the dwellers beside its banks are fond of calling it—that Frank Kingston first made the discovery of his own existence and of the world around him. He at once proceeded to make himself master of the situation, and so long as he confined his efforts to the limits of his own home he met with an encouraging degree of success; for he was an only child, and, his father's occupation requiring him to be away from home a large part of the year, his mother could hardly be severely blamed if she permitted her boy to have a good deal of his own way.

In the result, however, he was not spoiled. He came of sturdy, sensible stock, and had inherited some of the best qualities from both sides of the house. To his mother he owed his fair curly hair, his deep blue, honest eyes, his impulsive and tender heart; to his father, his strong symmetrical figure, his quick brain, and his eager ambition. He was a good-looking, if not strikingly handsome, boy, and carried himself in an alert, active way that made a good impression on one at the start. He had a quick temper that would flash out hotly if he were provoked, and at such times he would do and say things for which he was heartily sorry afterwards. But from those hateful qualities that we call malice, rancour, and sullenness he was absolutely free. To "have it out" and then shake hands and forget all about it—that was his way of dealing with a disagreement. Boys built on these lines are always popular among their comrades, and Frank was no exception. In fact, if one of those amicable contests as to the most popular personage, now so much in vogue at fairs and bazaars, were to have been held in Calumet school, the probabilities were all in favour of Frank coming out at the head of the poll.

But better, because more enduring than all these good qualities of body, head, and heart that formed Frank's sole fortune in the world, was the thorough religious training upon which they were based. His mother had left a Christian household to help her husband to found a new home in the great Canadian timberland; and this new home had ever been a sweet, serene centre of light and love. While Calumet was little more than a straggling collection of unlovely frame cottages, and too small to have a church and pastor of its own, the hard-working Christian minister who managed to make his way thither once a month or so, to hold service in the little schoolroom, was always sure of the heartiest kind of a welcome, and the daintiest dinner possible in that out-of-the-way place, at Mrs. Kingston's cozy cottage.— And thus Frank had been brought into friendly relations with the "men in black" from the start, with the good result of causing him to love and respect these zealous home missionaries, instead of shrinking from them in vague repugnance, as did many of his companions who had not his opportunities. —

When he grew old enough to be trusted, it was his proud privilege to take the minister's tired horse to water and to fill the rack with sweet hay for his refreshment before they all went off to the service together; and very frequently when the minister was leaving he would take Frank up beside him for a drive as far as the cross-roads, not losing the chance to say a kindly and encouraging word or two that might help the little fellow heavenward.

In due time the settlement so prospered and expanded that a little church was established there, and great was the delight of Mrs. Kingston when Calumet had its minister, to whom she continued to be a most effective helper. This love for the church and its workers, which was more manifest in her than in her husband—for, although he thought and felt alike with her, he was a reserved, undemonstrative man—Mrs. Kingston sought by every wise means to instil into her only son; and she had much success. Religion had no terrors for him. He had never thought of it as a gloomy, joy-dispelling influence that would make him a long-faced "softy." Not a bit of it. His father was religious; and who was stronger, braver, or more manly than his father? His mother was a pious woman; and who could laugh more cheerily or romp more merrily than his mother? The ministers who came to the house were men of God; and yet they were full of life and spirits, and dinner never seemed more delightful than when they sat at the table. No, indeed! You would have had a hard job to persuade Frank Kingston that you lost anything by being religious. He knew far better than that; and while of course he was too thorough a boy, with all a boy's hasty, hearty, impulsive ways, to do everything "decently and in order," and would kick over the traces, so to speak, sometimes, and give rather startling exhibitions of temper, still in the main and at heart he was a sturdy little Christian, who, when the storm was over, felt more sorry and remembered it longer than did anybody else.

Out of the way as Calumet might seem to city folk, yet the boys of the place managed to have a very good time. There were nearly a hundred of them, ranging in age from seven years to seventeen, attending the school which stood in the centre of a big lot at the western end of the village, and with swimming, boating, lacrosse, and baseball in summer, and skating, snow-shoeing, and tobogganing in winter, they never lacked for fun. Frank was expert in all these sports. Some of the boys might excel him at one or another of them, but not one of his companions could beat him in an all-round contest. This was due in part to the strength and symmetry of his frame, and in part to that spirit of thoroughness which characterized all he undertook. There was nothing half-way about him. He put his whole soul into everything that interested him, and, so far as play was concerned, at fifteen years of age he could swim, run, handle a lacrosse, hit a base-ball, skim over the ice on skates, or over snow on snow-shoes, with a dexterity that gave himself a vast amount of pleasure and his parents a good deal of pride in him.

Nor was he behindhand as regarded the training of his mind. Mr. Warren, the head teacher of the Calumet school, regarded him favourably as one of his best and brightest pupils, and it was not often that the "roll of honour" failed to contain the name of Frank Kingston. At the midsummer closing of the school it was Mr. Warren's practice to award a number of simple prizes to the pupils whose record throughout the half-year had been highest in the different subjects, and year after year Frank had won a goodly share of these trophies, which were always books, so that now there was a shelf in his room upon which stood in attractive array Livingstone's "Travels," Ballantyne's "Hudson Bay," Kingsley's "Westward Ho!" side by side with "Robinson Crusoe," "Pilgrim's Progress," and "Tom Brown at Rugby." Frank knew these books almost by heart, yet never wearied of turning to them again and again. He drew inspiration from them. They helped to mould his character, although of this he was hardly conscious, and they filled his soul with a longing for adventure and enterprise that no ordinary everyday career could satisfy. He looked forward eagerly to the time when he would take a man's part in life and attempt and achieve notable deeds. With Amyas Leigh he traversed the tropical wilderness of Southern America, or with the "Young Fur Traders" the hard-frozen wastes of the boundless North, and he burned to emulate their brave doings. He little knew, as he indulged in these boyish imaginations, that the time was not far off when the call would come to him to begin life in dead earnest on his own account, and with as many obstacles to be overcome in his way as had any of his favourite heroes in theirs.

Mr. Kingston was at home only during the summer season. The long cold winter months were spent by him at the "depot," many miles off in the heart of the forest, or at the "shanties" that were connected with it. At rare intervals during the winter he might manage to get home for a Sunday, but that was all his wife and son saw of him until the spring time. When the "drive" of the logs that represented the winter's work was over, he returned to them, to remain until the falling of the leaves recalled him to the forest. Frank loved and admired his father to the utmost of his ability; and when in his coolest, calmest moods he realized that there was small possibility of his ever sailing the Spanish main like Amyas Leigh, or exploring the interior of Africa like Livingstone, he felt quite settled in his own mind that, following in his father's footsteps, he would adopt lumbering as his business. 'Tis true, his father was only an agent or foreman, and might never be anything more; but even that was not to be despised, and then, with a little extra good fortune, he might in time become an owner of "limits" and mills himself. Why not? Many another boy had thus risen into wealth and importance. He had at least the right to try.

Fifteen in October, and in the highest class, this was to be Frank's last winter at school; and before leaving for the woods his father had enjoined upon him to make the best of it, as after the summer holidays were over he would have to "cease learning, and begin earning." Frank was rather glad to hear this. He was beginning to think he had grown too big for school, and ought to be doing something more directly remunerative. Poor boy! Could he have guessed that those were the last words he would hear from his dear father's lips, how differently would they have affected him! Calumet never saw Mr. Kingston again. In returning alone to the depot from a distant shanty, he was caught in a fierce and sudden snowstorm. The little-travelled road through the forest was soon obliterated. Blinded and bewildered by the pitiless storm beating in their faces, both man and beast lost their way, and, wandering about until all strength was spent, lay down to die in the drifts that quickly hid their bodies from sight. It was many days before they were found, lying together, close wrapped in their winding-sheet of snow.

Mrs. Kingston bore the dreadful trial with the fortitude and submissive grace that only a serene and unmurmuring faith can give. Frank was more demonstrative in his grief, and disposed to rebel against so cruel a calamity. But his mother calmed and inspired him, and when the first numbing force of the blow had passed away, they took counsel together as to the future. This was dark and uncertain enough. All that was left to them was the little cottage in which they lived. Mr. Kingston's salary had not been large, and only by careful management had the house been secured. Of kind and sympathizing friends there was no lack, but they were mostly people in moderate circumstances, like themselves, from whom nothing more than sympathy could be expected.

There was no alternative but that Frank should begin at once to earn his own living, and thus the conversation came about with which this chapter began, and which brought forth the reply from Frank that evidently gave his mother deep concern.

CHAPTER II.

THE CHOICE OF AN OCCUPATION.

THE fact was that Mrs. Kingston felt a strong repugnance to her son's following in his father's footsteps, so far as his occupation was concerned. She dreaded the danger that was inseparable from it, and shrank from the idea of giving up the boy, whose company was now the chief delight of her life, for all the long winter months that would be so dreary without him.

Frank had some inkling of his mother's feelings, but, boy like, thought of them as only the natural nervousness of womankind; and his heart being set upon going to the woods, he was not very open to argument.

"Why don't you want me to go lumbering, mother?" he inquired in a tone that had a touch of petulance in it. "I've got to do something for myself, and I detest shopkeeping. It's not in my line at all. Fellows like Tom Clemon and Jack Stoner may find it suits them, but I can't bear the idea of being shut up in a shop or office all day. I want to be out of doors. That's the kind of life for me."

Mrs. Kingston gave a sigh that was a presage of defeat as she regarded her son standing before her, his handsome face flushed with eagerness and his eyes flashing with determination.

"But, Frank dear," said she gently, "have you thought how dreadfully lonely it will be for me living all alone here during the long winter—your father gone from me, and you away off in the woods, where I can never get to you or you to me?"

The flush on Frank's face deepened and extended until it covered forehead and neck with its crimson glow. He had not taken this view of the case into consideration before, and his tender heart reproached him for so forgetting his mother while laying out his own plans. He sprang forward, and kneeling down beside the lounge, threw his arms about his mother's neck and clasped her fondly, finding it hard to keep the tears back as he said,—

"You dear, darling mother! I have been selfish. I should have thought how lonely it would be for you in the winter time."

22 THE CHOICE OF AN OCCUPATION.

Mrs. Kingston returned the embrace with no less fervour, and as usually happens where the other side seems to be giving way, began to weaken somewhat herself, and to feel a little doubtful as to whether, after all, it would be right to oppose her son's wishes when his inclinations toward the occupation he had chosen were evidently so very decided.

"Well, Frank dear," she said after a pause, while Frank looked at her expectantly, "I don't want to be selfish either. If it were not for the way we lost your father, perhaps I should not have such a dread of the woods for you; and no doubt even then it is foolish for me to give way to it. We won't decide the matter now. If you do go to the woods, it won't be until the autumn, and perhaps during the summer something will turn up that will please us better. We will leave the matter in God's hands. He will bring it to pass in the way that will be best for us both, I am confident."

So with that understanding the matter rested, although of course it was continually being referred to as the weeks slipped by and the summer waxed and waned. Although Frank felt quite convinced in his own mind that he was not cut out for a position behind a desk or counter, he determined to make the

THE CHOICE OF AN OCCUPATION.

experiment, and accordingly applied to Squire Eagleson, who kept the principal shop and was the "big man" of the village, for a place in his establishment. Summer being the squire's busy season, and Frank being well known to him, he was glad enough to add to his small staff of clerks so promising a recruit, especially as, taking advantage of the boy's ignorance of business affairs, he was able to engage him at wages much below his actual worth to him This the worthy squire regarded as quite a fine stroke of business, and told it to his wife with great gusto, rubbing his fat hands complacently together as he chuckled over his shrewdness.

"Bright boy that Frank Kingston! Writes a good fist, and can run up a row of figures like smoke. Mighty civil, too, and sharp. And all for seven shillings a week! Ha, ha, ha! Wish I could make as good a bargain as that every day." And the squire looked the picture of virtuous content as he leaned back in his big chair to enjoy the situation.

Mrs. Eagleson did not often venture to intermeddle in her husband's business affairs, although frequently she became aware of things which she could not reconcile with her conscience. But this time she was moved to speak by an impulse she could not control.

She knew the Kingstons, and had always thought well of them. Mrs. Kingston seemed to her in many respects a model woman, who deserved well of everybody; and that her husband, who was so well-to-do, should take any advantage of these worthy people who had so little, touched her to the quick. There was a bright spot on the centre of her pale cheeks and an unaccustomed ring in her voice, as she exclaimed, with a sharpness that made her husband give quite a start of surprise,—

"Do you mean to tell me, Daniel, that you've been mean enough to take advantage of that boy who has to support his widowed mother, and to hire him for half the wages he's worth, just because he didn't know any better? And then you come home here and boast of it! Have you no conscience?"

The squire was so taken aback by this unexpected attack that at first he hardly knew how to meet it. Should he lecture his wife for her presumption in meddling in his affairs, which were quite beyond her comprehension as a woman, or should he make light of the matter and laugh it off? After a moment's reflection he decided on the latter course.

"Hoity, toity, Mrs. Eagleson! but what's set you so suddenly on fire? Business is business, you know, and if Frank Kingston did not know enough to ask for more wages, it wasn't my concern to enlighten him."

Mrs. Eagleson rose from her chair and came over and stood in front of her husband, pointing her long, thin forefinger at him as, with a trembling yet scornful voice, she addressed him thus,—

"Daniel, how you can kneel down and ask the blessing of God upon such doings is beyond me, or how your head can lie easy on your pillow when you know that you are taking the bread out of that poor lone widow's mouth it is not for me to say. But this I will say, whether you like it or not: if you are not ashamed of yourself, I am for you." And before the now much-disturbed squire had time to say another word in his defence the speaker had swept indignantly out of his presence and hastened to her own room, there to throw herself down upon the bed and burst into a passion of tears, for she was at best but a weak-nerved woman.

Left to himself, the squire shifted about uneasily in his chair, and then rose and stumped angrily to the window.

"What does she know about business?" he muttered. "If she were to have her own way at the store, she'd ruin me in a twelvemonth."

Yet Mrs. Eagleson's brave outburst was not in vain. Somehow or other after it the squire never felt comfortable in his mind until, much to Frank's surprise and delight, he one day called him to him, and, with an air of great generosity and patronage, said,—

"See here, my lad. You seem to be doing your work real well, so I am going to give you half-a-crown a week more just to encourage you, and then if a little extra work comes along "—for autumn was approaching—" ye won't mind tackling it with a good will; eh ?"

Frank thanked his employer very heartily, and this unexpected increase of earnings and his mother's joy over it for a time almost reconciled him to the work at the shop, which he liked less and less the longer he was at it.

The fact of the matter was, a place behind the counter was uncongenial to him in many ways. There was too much in-doors about it, to begin with. From early morning until late evening he had to be at his post, with brief intervals for meals; and the colour was leaving his cheeks, and his muscles were growing slack and soft, owing to the constant confinement.

But this was the least of his troubles. A still

THE CHOICE OF AN OCCUPATION.

more serious matter was that his conscience did not suffer him to take kindly to the " tricks of the trade," in which his employer was a " passed master " and his fellow-clerks very promising pupils. He could not find it in his heart to depreciate the quality of Widow Perkins's butter, or to cajole unwary Sam Struthers, from the backlands, into taking a shop-worn remnant for the new dress his wife had so carefully commissioned him to buy. His idea of trade was that you should deal with others as fairly as you would have them deal with you; and while, of course, according to the squire's philosophy, you could never make a full purse that way, still you could at least have a clear conscience, which surely was the more desirable after all.

The squire had noticed Frank's " pernickety nonsense," as he was pleased to call it, and at first gave him several broad hints as to the better mode of doing business; but finding that the lad was firm, and would no doubt give up his place rather than learn these " business ways," he had the good sense to let him alone, finding in his quickness, fidelity, and attention to his work sufficient compensation for this deficiency in bargaining acumen.

"You'll be content to stay at the shop now, won't

you, Frank?" said his mother as they talked over the welcome and much-needed rise of salary.

"It does seem to make it easier to stay, mother," answered Frank. "But——" And he gave a big sigh, and stopped.

"But what, dear?" asked Mrs. Kingston, tenderly.

Frank was slow in answering. He evidently felt reluctant to bring up the matter again, and yet his mind was full of it.

"But what, Frank?" repeated his mother, taking his hands in hers and looking earnestly into his face.

"Well, mother, it's no use pretending. I'm not cut out for keeping shop, and I'll never be much good at it. I don't like being in-doors all day. And then, if you want to get on, you've got to do all sorts of things that are nothing else but downright mean; and I don't like that either." And then Frank went on to tell of some of the tricks and stratagems the squire or the other clerks would resort to in order to make a good bargain.

Mrs. Kingston listened with profound attention. More than once of late, as she noticed her son's growing pallor and loss of spirits, she had asked herself whether she were not doing wrong in seeking to turn him aside from the life for which he longed; and now that he was finding fresh and fatal objections to the occupation he had chosen in deference to her wishes, she began to relent of her insistence, and to feel more disposed to discuss the question again. But before doing so she wished to ask the advice of a friend in whom she placed much confidence, and so for the present she contented herself with applauding Frank for his conscientiousness, and assuring him that she would a thousand times rather have him always poor than grow rich after the same fashion as Squire Eagleson.

The friend whose advice Mrs. Kingston wished to take was her husband's successor as foreman at the depot for the lumber camps—a sensible, steady, reliable young man, who had risen to his present position by process of promotion from the bottom, and who was therefore well qualified to give her just the counsel she desired. At the first opportunity, therefore, she went over to Mr. Stewart's cottage, and, finding him at home, opened her heart fully to him. Mr. Stewart, or Alec Stewart, as he was generally called, listened with ready sympathy to what Mrs. Kingston had to say, and showed much interest in the matter, for he had held a high opinion of his former chief, and knew Frank well enough to admire his spirit and character.

"Well, you see, Mrs. Kingston, it's just this way," said he, when his visitor had stated the case upon which she wanted his opinion: "if Frank's got his heart so set upon going into the woods, I don't know as there's any use trying to cross him. He won't take kindly to anything else while he's thinking of that; and he'd a big sight better be a good lumberman than a poor clerk, don't you think?"

Mrs. Kingston felt the force of this reasoning, yet could hardly make up her mind to yield to it at once.

"But, Mr. Stewart," she urged, "it may only be a boyish notion of Frank's. He thinks, perhaps, he'd like it because that's what his father was before him, and then he may find his mistake."

"Well, Mrs. Kingston," replied Mr. Stewart, "if you think there's any chance of that being the case, we can settle the question right enough in this way:— Let Frank come to the woods with me this winter. I will give him a berth as chore-boy in one of the camps; and if that doesn't sicken him of the business, then all I can say is you'd better let the lad have his will."

Mrs. Kingston sighed.

"I suppose you're right. I don't quite like the idea of his being chore-boy; but if he's really in earnest, there's no better way of proving him."

Now Frank knew well enough how humble was the position of "chore-boy" in a lumber camp. It meant that he would be the boy-of-all-work; that he would have to be up long before dawn, and be one of the last in the camp to get into his bunk; that he would have to help the cook, take messages for the foreman, be obliging to the men, and altogether do his best to be generally useful. Yet he did not shrink from the prospect. The idea of release from the uncongenial routine of shopkeeping filled him with happiness, and his mother was almost reconciled to letting him go from her, so marked was the change in his spirits.

CHAPTER III.

OFF TO THE WOODS.

SEPTEMBER, the finest of all the months in the Canadian calendar, was at hand, as the sumac and the maple took evident delight in telling by their lovely tints of red and gold, and the hot, enervating breath of summer had yielded to the inspiring coolness of early autumn. The village of Calumet fairly bubbled over with business and bustle. Preparations for the winter's work were being made on all sides. During the course of the next two weeks or so a large number of men would be leaving their homes for the lumber camps, and the chief subject of conversation in all circles was the fascinating and romantic occupation in which they were engaged

No one was more busy than Mrs. Kingston. Even if her son was to be only a chore-boy, his equipment should be as comfortable and complete as though he were going to be a foreman. She knew very well that Jack Frost has no compunctions about sending the thermometer away down thirty or forty degrees below zero in those far-away forest depths; and whatever other hardships Frank might be called upon to endure, it was very well settled in her mind that he should not suffer for lack of warm clothing. Accordingly, the knitting-needles and sewing-needles had been plied industriously from the day his going into the woods was decided upon; and now that the time for departure drew near, the result was to be seen in a chest filled with such thick warm stockings, shirts, mittens, and comforters, besides a good outfit of other clothing, that Frank, looking them over with a keen appreciation of their merits and of the loving skill they evidenced, turned to his mother, saying, with a grateful smile,—

"Why, mother, you've fitted me out as though I were going to the North Pole."

"You'll need them all, my dear, before the winter's over," said Mrs. Kingston, the tears rising in her eyes, as involuntarily she thought of how the cruel cold had taken from her the father of the bright, hopeful boy before her. "Your father never thought I provided too many warm things for him."

Frank was in great spirits. He had resigned his

clerkship at Squire Eagleson's, much to that worthy merchant's regret. The squire looked upon him as a very foolish fellow to give up a position in his shop, where he had such good opportunities of learning business ways, in order to go "galivanting off to the woods," where his good writing and correct figuring would be of no account.

Frank said nothing about his decided objections to the squire's ideas of business ways and methods, but contented himself with stating respectfully his strong preference for out-door life, and his intention to make lumbering his occupation, as it had been his father's before him.

"Well, well, my lad," said the squire, when he saw there was no moving him, "have your own way. I reckon you'll be glad enough to come back to me in the spring. One winter in the camps will be all you'll want."

Frank left the squire, saying to himself as he went out from the shop :—

"If I do get sick of the camp and want a situation in the spring, this is not the place I'll come to for it; you can depend upon that, Squire Eagleson. Many thanks to you, all the same."

Mr. Stewart was going up to the depot the first

week in September, to get matters in readiness for the men who would follow him a week later, and much to Frank's satisfaction he announced that he would take him along if he could be ready in time. Thanks to Mrs. Kingston's being of the fore-handed kind, nothing was lacking in her son's preparations, and the day of departure was anticipated with great eagerness by him, and with much sinking of heart by her.

The evening previous mother and son had a long talk together, in the course of which she impressed upon him the absolute importance of his making no disguise of his religious principles.

"You'll be the youngest in the camp, perhaps, Frank darling, and it will, no doubt, be very hard for you to read your Bible and say your prayers, as you've always done here at home. But the braver you are about it at first, the easier it'll be in the end. Take your stand at the very start. Let the shanty men see that you're not afraid to confess yourself a Christian, and rough and wicked as they may be, never fear but they'll respect you for it."

Mrs. Kingston spoke with an earnestness and emphasis that went straight to Frank's heart. He had perfect faith in his mother. In his eyes she was without fault or failing, and he knew very well that she was asking nothing of him that she was not altogether ready to do herself, were she to be put in his place. Not only so. His own shrewd sense confirmed the wisdom of her words. There could be no half-way position for him at the lumber camp; no half-hearted serving of God would be of any use there. He must take Caleb for his pattern, and follow the Lord wholly. His voice was low, but full of quiet determination, as he answered,—

"I know it, mother. It won't be easy, but I'm not afraid. I'll begin fair and let the others know just where I stand, and they may say or do what they like."

Mrs. Kingston needed no further assurance to make her mind quite easy upon this point; and she took no small comfort from the thought that, faithful and consistent as she felt so confident Frank would be, despite the many trials and temptations inseparable from his new sphere of life, he could hardly fail to exercise some good influence upon those about him, and perhaps prove a very decided power for good among the rough men of the lumber camp.

The day of departure dawned clear and bright. The air was cool and bracing, the ground glistened with the heavy autumn dew that the sun had not yet had time to drink up, and the village was not fairly astir for the day when Mr. Stewart drove up to Mrs. Kingston's door for his young passenger. He was not kept long waiting, for Frank had been ready fully half-an-hour beforehand, and all that remained to be done was to bid his mother "good-bye," until he should return with the spring floods. Overflowing with joy as he was at the realization of his desire, yet he was too fond a son not to feel keenly the parting with his mother, and he bustled about very vigorously, stowing away his things in the back of the waggon, as the best way of keeping himself under control.

He had a good deal of luggage for a boy. First of all, there was his chest packed tight with warm clothing; then another box heavy with cake, preserves, pickles, and other home-made dainties, wherewith to vary the monotony of shanty fare; then a big bundle containing a wool mattress, a pillow, two pairs of heavy blankets, and a thick comforter to insure his sleep being undisturbed by saucy Jack Frost; and finally, a narrow box made by his own father to carry the light rifle that always accompanied him, together with a plentiful supply of ammunition. In this box

Frank was particularly interested, for he had learned to handle this rifle pretty well during the summer, and looked forward to accomplishing great things with it when he got into the woods.

Mr. Stewart laughed when he saw all that Frank was taking with him.

"I guess you'll be the swell of the camp, and make all the other fellows wish they had a mother to fit them out. It's a fortunate thing my waggon's roomy, or we'd have to leave some of your stuff to come up by one of the teams," said he.

Mrs. Kingston was about to make apologies for the size of Frank's outfit, but Mr. Stewart stopped her.

"It's all right, Mrs. Kingston. The lad might just as well be comfortable as not. He'll have plenty of roughing it, anyway. And now we've got it all on board, we must be starting."

The moment Mrs. Kingston dreaded had now come. Throwing her arms around Frank's neck, she clasped him passionately to her heart again and again, and then, tearing herself away from him, rushed up the steps as if she dared not trust herself any longer. Gulping down the big lump that rose into his throat, Frank sprang up beside Mr. Stewart, and the next moment they were off. But before they turned the corner Frank, looking back, caught sight of his mother standing in the doorway, and taking off his cap he gave her a farewell salute, calling out rather huskily his last "good-bye" as the swiftly-moving waggon bore him away.

Mr. Stewart took much pride in his turn-out, and with good reason; for there was not a finer pair of horses in Calumet than those that were now trotting along before him, as if the well-filled waggon to which they were attached was no impediment whatever. His work required him to be much upon the road in all seasons, and he considered it well worth his while to make the business of driving about as pleasant as possible. The horses were iron-grays, beautifully matched in size, shape, and speed; the harness sparkled with bright brass mountings; and the waggon, a kind of express, with specially strong springs and comfortable seat, had abundant room for passengers and luggage.

As they rattled along the village street there were many shouts of "Good-bye, Frank," and "Good luck to you," from shop and sidewalk; for everybody knew Frank's destination, and there were none that did not wish him well, whatever might be their opinion of the wisdom of his action. In responding to these expressions of good-will, Frank found timely relief for the feelings stirred by the parting with his mother, and before the impatient grays had breasted the hill which began where the village ended he had quite regained his customary good spirits, and was ready to reply brightly enough to Mr. Stewart's remarks.

"Well, Frank, you've put your hand to the plough now, as the Scripture says, and you mustn't turn back on any account, or all the village will be laughing at you," he said, scanning his companion closely.

"Not much fear of that, Mr. Stewart," answered Frank firmly. "Calumet won't see me again until next spring. Whether I like the lumbering or not, I'm going to stick out the winter, anyway; you see if I don't."

"I haven't much fear of you, my boy," returned Mr. Stewart, "even if you do find shanty life a good deal rougher than you may have imagined. You'll have to fight your own way, you know. I shan't be around much, and the other men will all be strangers at first; but just you do what you know and feel to be right without minding the others, and they won't bother you long, but will respect you for having a conscience and the pluck to obey it. As for your work, it'll seem pretty heavy and hard at the start; but you've got lots of grit, and it won't take you long to get used to it."

Frank listened attentively to Mr. Stewart's kindly, sensible advice, and had many questions to ask him as the speedy horses bore them further and further away from Calumet. The farms, which at first had followed one another in close succession, grew more widely apart, and finally ended altogether before many miles of the dusty road had been covered, and thenceforward their way ran through unbroken woods, not the stately " forest primeval " but the scrubby " second growth," from which those who have never been into the heart of the leafy wilderness can form but a poor conception of the grandeur to which trees can attain.

About mid-day they halted at a lonely log-house which served as a sort of inn or resting-place, the proprietor finding compensation for the dreariness of his situation in the large profit derived from an illegal but thriving traffic in liquor. A more unkempt, unattractive establishment could hardly be imagined, and if rumour was to be relied upon, it had good reason to be haunted by more than one untimely ghost.

"A wretched den!" said Mr. Stewart, as he drew up before the door. "I wouldn't think of stopping here for a moment but for the horses. But we may as well go in and see if old Pierre can get us a decent bite to eat."

The horses having been attended to, the travellers entered the house, where they found Pierre, the proprietor, dozing on his bar, a bloated, blear-eyed creature, who evidently would have much preferred making them drunk with his vile whisky to preparing them any pretence for a dinner. But they firmly declined his liquor, so muttering unintelligibly to himself he shambled off to obey their behests. After some delay they succeeded in getting a miserable meal of some kind; and then, the horses being sufficiently rested, they set off once more at a good pace, not halting again until, just before sundown, they arrived at the depot, where the first stage of their journey ended.

This depot was simply a large farm set in the midst of a wilderness of trees, and forming a centre from which some half-dozen shanties, or lumber camps, placed at different distances in the depths of the forest that stretched away interminably north, south, east, and west, were supplied with all that was necessary for their maintenance. Besides the ordinary farm buildings, there was another which served as a sort of a shop or warehouse, being filled with a stock of axes, saws, blankets, boots, beef, pork, tea, sugar, molasses, flour, and so forth, for the use of the lumbermen. This was Mr. Stewart's headquarters, and as the tired horses drew up before the door he tossed the reins over their backs, saying,—

"Here we are, Frank. You'll stay here until your gang is made up. To-morrow morning I'll introduce you to some of your mates."

CHAPTER IV.

THE BUILDING OF THE SHANTY.

FRANK looked about him with quick curiosity, expecting to see some of the men in whose society he was to spend the winter. But there were only the farm-hands lounging listlessly about, their day's work being over, and they had nothing to do except to smoke their pipes and wait for nightfall, when they would lounge off to bed.

The shantymen had not yet arrived, Mr. Stewart always making a point of being at the depot some days in advance of them, in order to have plenty of time to prepare his plans for the winter campaign. Noting Frank's inquiring look, he laughed, and said,—

"Oh, there are none of them here yet—we're the first on the field—but by the end of the week there'll be more than a hundred men here."

A day or two later the first batch made their ap-

THE BUILDING OF THE SHANTY. 45

pearance, coming up by the heavy teams that they would take with them into the woods; and each day brought a fresh contingent, until by the time Mr. Stewart had mentioned the farm fairly swarmed with them, and it became necessary for this human hive to imitate the bees and send off its superfluous inhabitants without delay.

They were a rough, noisy, strange-looking lot of men, and Frank, whose acquaintance with the shanty-men had been limited to seeing them in small groups as they passed through Calumet in the autumn and spring, on their way to and from the camps, meeting them now for the first time in such large numbers, could not help some inward shrinking of soul as he noted their uncouth ways and listened to their oath-besprinkled talk. They were " all sorts and conditions of men "—habitants who could not speak a word of English, and Irishmen who could not speak a word of French; shrewd Scotchmen, chary of tongue and reserved of manner, and loquacious half-breeds, ready for song, or story, or fight, according to the humour of the moment. Here and there were dusky skins and prominent features that betrayed a close connection with the aboriginal owners of this continent. Almost all had come from the big sawmills away down the river, or from some other equally arduous employment, and were glad of the chance of a few days' respite from work while Mr. Stewart was dividing them up and making the necessary arrangements for the winter's work.

Frank mingled freely with them, scraping acquaintance with those who seemed disposed to be friendly, and whenever he came across one with an honest, pleasant, prepossessing face, hoping very much that he would be a member of his gang. He was much impressed by the fact that he was evidently the youngest member of the gathering, and did not fail to notice the sometimes curious, sometimes contemptuous, looks with which he was regarded by the fresh arrivals.

In the course of a few days matters were pretty well straightened out at the depot, and the gangs of men began to leave for the different camps. Mr. Stewart had promised Frank that he would take care to put him under a foreman who would treat him well; and when one evening he was called into the office and introduced to a tall, powerful, grave-looking man, with heavy brown beard and deep voice, Mr. Stewart said,—

" Here is Frank Kingston, Dan; Jack's only son,

THE BUILDING OF THE SHANTY. 47

you know. He's set his heart on lumbering, and I'm going to let him try it for a winter."

Frank scrutinized the man called Dan very closely as Mr. Stewart continued,—

"I'm going to send him up to the Kippewa camp with you, Dan. There's nobody'll look after him better than you will, for I know you thought a big sight of his father, and for his sake as well as mine you'll see that nothing happens to the lad."

Dan Johnston's face relaxed into a smile that showed there were rich depths of good nature beneath his rather stern exterior, for he was pleased at the compliment implied in the superintendent's words, and stretching out a mighty hand to Frank, he laid it on his shoulder in a kindly way, saying,—

"He seems a likely lad, Mr. Stewart, and a chip of the old block, if I'm not mistaken. I'll be right glad to have him with me. But what kind of work is he to go at? He seems rather light for chopping, doesn't he?"

Mr. Stewart gave a quizzical sort of glance at Frank as he replied,—

"Well, you see, Dan, I think myself he is too light for chopping, so I told him he'd have to be chore-boy for this winter, anyway."

A look of surprise came over Johnston's face, and, more to himself than the others, he muttered in a low tone,—

"Chore-boy, eh? Jack Kingston's son a chore-boy!" Then turning to Frank, he said aloud, "All right, my boy. There's nothing like beginning at the bottom if you want to learn the whole business. You must make up your mind to put in a pretty hard time, but I'll see you have fair play, anyway."

As Frank looked at the rugged, honest, determined face, and the stalwart frame, he felt thoroughly satisfied that in Dan Johnston he had a friend in whom he could place perfect confidence, and that Mr. Stewart's promise had been fully kept. The foreman then became quite sociable, and asked him many questions about his mother, and his life in Calumet, and his plans for the future, so that before they parted for the night Frank felt as if they were quite old friends instead of recent acquaintances.

The following morning Johnston was bestirring himself bright and early getting his men and stores together, and before noon a start was made for the Kippewa River, on whose southern bank a site had already been selected for the lumber camp which would be the centre of his operations for the winter.

Johnston's gang numbered fifty men all told, himself included, and they were in high spirits as they set out for their destination. The stores and tools were, of course, transported by waggon; but the men had to go on foot, and with fifteen miles of a rough forest road to cover before sundown, they struck a brisk pace as, in twos and threes and quartettes, they marched noisily along the dusty road.

"You stay by me, Frank," said the foreman, "and if your young legs happen to go back on you, you can have a lift on one of the teams until you're rested."

Frank felt in such fine trim that although he fully appreciated his big friend's thoughtfulness, he was rash enough to think he would not require to avail himself of it; but the next five miles showed him his mistake, and at the end of them he was very glad to jump upon one of the teams that happened to be passing, and in this way hastened over a good part of the remainder of the tramp.

As the odd-looking gang pushed forward steadily, if not in exactly martial order, Frank had a good opportunity of inspecting its members, and making in his own mind an estimate of their probable good or bad qualities as companions. In this he was much assisted by the foreman, who, in reply to his questions, gave him helpful bits of information about the different ones that attracted his attention. Fully one-half of the gang were French Canadians, dark-complexioned, black-haired, bright-eyed men, full of life and talk, their tongues going unceasingly as they plodded along in sociable groups. Of the remainder, some were Scotch, others Irish, the rest English. Upon the whole, they were quite a promising-looking lot of men; indeed, Johnston took very good care to have as little " poor stuff" as possible in his gang; for he had long held the reputation of turning out more logs at his camp than were cut at any other on the same "limits;" and this well-deserved fame he cherished very dearly.

Darkness was coming on apace, when at last a glad shout from the foremost group announced that the end of the journey was near; and in a few minutes more the whole band of tired men were resting their wearied limbs on the bank of the river near which the shanty was to be erected at once. The teams had arrived some time before them, and two large tents had been put up as temporary shelter; while brightly-burning fires and the appetizing fizzle of frying bacon joined with the wholesome aroma of

THE BUILDING OF THE SHANTY.   51

hot tea to make glad the hearts of the dusty, hungry pedestrians.

Frank enjoyed his open-air tea immensely. It was his first taste of real lumberman's life, and was undoubtedly a pleasant introduction to it; for the hard work would not begin until the morrow, and in the meantime everybody was still a-holidaying. So refreshing was the evening meal that, tired as all no doubt felt from their long tramp, they soon forgot it sufficiently to spend an hour or more in song and chorus that made the vast forest aisles re-echo with rough melody before they sank into the silence of slumber for the night.

At daybreak next morning Dan Johnston's stentorian voice aroused the sleepers, and Frank could hardly believe that he had taken more than twice forty winks at the most before the stirring shout of "Turn out! turn out! The work's waiting!" broke into his dreams and recalled him to life's realities. The morning was gray and chilly, the men looked sleepy and out of humour, and Johnston himself had a stern distant manner, or seemed to have, as after a wash at the river bank Frank approached him and reported himself for duty.

"Will you please to tell me what is to be my

work, Mr. Johnston?" said he, in quite a timid tone; for somehow or other there seemed to be a change in the atmosphere.

The foreman's face relaxed a little as he turned to answer him.

"You want to be set to work, eh? Well, that won't take long." And looking around among the moving men until he found the one he wanted, he raised his voice and called,—

"Hi, there, Baptiste! Come here a moment."

In response to the summons a short, stout, smooth-faced, and decidedly good-natured looking Frenchman, who had been busy at one of the fires, came over to the foreman.

"See here, Baptiste; this lad's to be your chore-boy this winter, and I don't want you to be too hard on him—*savez?* Let him have plenty of work, but not more than his share."

Baptiste examined Frank's sturdy figure with much the same smile of approval that he might bestow upon a fine capon that he was preparing for the pot, and murmured out something like,—

"*Bien, m'sieur.* I sall be easy wid him if ee's a good boy."

The foreman then said to Frank,—

THE BUILDING OF THE SHANTY.

"There, Frank, go with Baptiste, and he'll give you work enough."

So Frank went dutifully off with the Frenchman.

He soon found out what his work was to be. Baptiste was cook, and he was his assistant, not so much in the actual cooking, for Baptiste looked after that himself, but in the scouring of the pots and pans, the keeping up of the fires, the setting out of the food, and such other supplementary duties. Not very dignified or inspiring employment, certainly, especially for a boy "with a turn for books and figures." But Frank had come to the camp prepared to undertake, without a murmur, any work within his powers that might be given him, and he now went quietly and steadily at what was required of him.

As soon as breakfast was despatched, Johnston called the men together to give them directions about the building of the shanty, which was the first thing of all to be done; and having divided them up into parties, to each of which a different task was assigned, he set them at work without delay.

Frank was very glad that attention to his duties would not prevent his watching the others at theirs; for what could be more interesting than to study every stage of the erection of the building that was to be their shelter and home during the long winter months now rapidly approaching? It was a first experience for him, and nothing escaped his vigilant eye. This is the way he described the building of the shanty to his mother on his return to Calumet:—

"You see, mother, everybody except Baptiste and myself took a hand, and just worked like beavers. I wish you could have seen the men. And Mr. Johnston—why, he was in two places at once most of the time, or at least seemed to be! It was grand fun watching them. The first thing they did was to cut down a lot of trees—splendid big fellows, that would make the trees round here look pretty small, I can tell you. Then they chopped off all the branches and cut up the trunks into the lengths that suited, and laid them one on the top of the other until they made a wall about as high as Mr. Johnston, or perhaps higher, in the shape of one big room forty feet long by thirty feet wide, Mr. Johnston said. It looked very funny then—just like a huge pig-pen, with no windows and only one door—on the side that faced the river. Next day they laid long timbers across the top of the wall, resting them in the middle on four great posts they called 'scoop-bearers.' Funny name, isn't it? But they called them that because

THE BUILDING OF THE SHANTY.

they bear the 'scoops' that make the roof; and a grand roof it is, I tell you. The scoops are small logs hollowed out on one side and flat on the other; and they lay them on the cross timbers in such a way that the edges of one fit into the hollows of two others, so that the rain hasn't a chance to get in, no matter how hard it tries. Next thing they made the floor; and that wasn't a hard job, for they just made logs flat on two sides and laid them on the ground, so that it was a pretty rough sort of a floor. All the cracks were stuffed tight with moss and mud, and a big bank of earth thrown up around the bottom of the wall to keep the draught out.

"But you should have seen the beds, or 'bunks,' as they called them, for the men. I don't believe you could ever sleep on them. They were nothing but board platforms all around three sides of the room, built on a slant so that your head was higher than your feet; so you see I'd have had nothing better than the soft side of a plank for a mattress if you hadn't fitted me out with one. And when the other fellows saw how snug I was, they vowed they'd have a soft bed too; so what do you think they did? They gathered an immense quantity of hemlock branches—little soft ones, you know—and spread them thick over the boards, and then they laid blankets over that and made a really fine mattress for all. So that, you see, I quite set the fashion. The last thing to be made was the fireplace, which has the very queer name of 'caboose,' and is queerer than its name. It is right in the middle of the room, not at one end, and is as big as a small room by itself. First of all, a great bank of stones and sand is laid on the floor, kept together by boards at the edges; then a large square hole is cut in the roof above, and a wooden chimney built on the top of it; and then at two of the corners cranes to hold the pots are fixed, and the caboose is complete. And oh, mother, such roaring big fires as were always going in it after the cold came—all night long, you know; and sometimes I had to stay awake to keep the fire from going out, which wasn't much fun, but, of course, I had to take my turn. So now, mother, you ought to have a pretty good idea of what our shanty was like; for, besides a table and our chests, there was nothing much else in it to describe."

Such were Frank Kingston's surroundings as he entered upon the humble and laborious duties of chore-boy in Camp Kippewa, not attempting to conceal from himself that he would much rather be a

THE BUILDING OF THE SHANTY. 57

chopper or teamster or road-maker, but with his mind fully fixed upon doing his work, however uncongenial it might be, cheerfully and faithfully for one winter at least, feeling confident that if he did he would not be chore-boy for long, but would in due time be promoted to some more dignified and attractive position.

CHAPTER V.

STANDING FIRE.

THE shanty finished, a huge mass of wood cut into convenient lengths and piled near the door, a smooth road made down to the river-bank, the store-house filled with barrels of pork and flour and beans and chests of tea, the stable for the score of horses, put up after much the same architectural design as the shanty, and then the lumber camp was complete, and the men were free to address themselves to the business that had brought them so far.

As Frank looked around him at the magnificent forests into whose heart they had penetrated, and tried with his eyes to measure the height of the splendid trees that towered above his head on every side, he found himself touched with a feeling of sympathy for them—as if it seemed a shame to humble the pride of those silvan monarchs by bringing them crashing to the earth. And then this feeling gave way to another; and as he watched the expert choppers swinging their bright axes in steady rhythm, and adding wound to wound in the gaping trunk so skilfully that the defenceless monster fell just where they wished, his heart thrilled with pride at man's easy victory over nature, and he longed to seize an axe himself and attack the forest on his own account.

He had plenty of axe work as it was, but of a much more prosaic kind. An important part of his duty consisted in keeping up the great fire that roared and crackled unceasingly in the caboose. The appetite of this fire seemed unappeasable, and many a time did his arms and legs grow weary in ministering to its wants. Sometimes, when all his other work was done, he would go out to the wood-pile, and selecting the thickest and toughest-looking logs, arrange them upon the hearth so that they might take as long as possible to burn; and then, congratulating himself that he had secured some respite from toil, get out his rifle for a little practice at a mark, or would open one of the few books he had brought with him. But it seemed to him he would hardly have more than one shot at the mark, or get through half-a-dozen pages, before Baptiste's thick voice would be heard calling out,—

"Francois, Francois! Ver is yer? Some more wood, k'vick!" And with a groan poor Frank would have to put away the rifle or book and return to the wood-pile.

"I suppose I'm what the Bible calls a hewer of wood and a drawer of water," he would say to himself; for hardly less onerous than the task of keeping the fire in fuel was that of keeping well filled the two water-barrels that stood on either side of the door—one for the thirsty shantymen, the other for Baptiste's culinary needs.

The season's work once well started, it went forward with commendable steadiness and vigour under Foreman Johnston's strict and energetic management. He was admirably suited for his difficult position. His grave, reserved manner rendered impossible that familiarity which is so apt to breed contempt, while his thorough mastery of all the secrets of woodcraft, his great physical strength, and his absolute fearlessness in the face of any peril, combined to make him a fit master for the strangely-assorted half-hundred of men now under his sole control. Frank held him in profound respect, and would have endured almost anything rather than seem unmanly or unheedful in his eyes. To win a word of commendation from those firm-set lips that said so little was the desire of his heart, and, feeling sure that it would come time enough, he stuck to his work bravely, quite winning good-natured Baptiste's heart by his prompt obedience to orders.

"You are a *bon garçon*, Francois," he would say, patting his shoulder with his plump palm. "Too good to be chore-boy; but not for long—eh, Francois? You be chopper *bientôt*, and then"—with an expressive wave of his hand to indicate the rapid flight of time—"you'll be foreman, like M'sieur Johnston, while Baptiste"—and the broad shoulders would rise in that meaning shrug which only Frenchmen can achieve—"poor Baptiste will be cook still."

Beginning with Johnston and Baptiste, Frank was rapidly making friends among his companions, and as he was soon to learn, much to his surprise and sorrow, some enemies too—or, rather, to be more correct, he was making the friends, but the enemies were making themselves; for he was to blame in small part, if at all, for their rising against him. There were all sorts and conditions of men, so far at least as character and disposition went, among the gang, and the evil element was fitly represented by a small group of inhabitants who recognized one Damase Deschenaux as their leader. This Damase made rather a striking figure. Although he scorned the suggestion as hotly as would a Southern planter the charge that negro blood darkened his veins, there was no doubt that some generations back the dusky wife of a *courier du bois* had mingled the Indian nature with the French. Unhappily for Damase, the result of his ancestral error was manifest in him; for, while bearing but little outward resemblance to his savage progenitor, he was at heart a veritable Indian.

Greedy, selfish, jealous, treacherous, quick to take offence and slow to forgive or forget, his presence in the Johnston gang was explained by his wonderful knowledge of the forest, his sure judgment in selecting good bunches of timber to be cut, and his intimate acquaintance with the course of the stream down which the logs would be floated in the spring.

Johnston had no liking for Damase, but found him too valuable to dispense with. This year, by chance, or possibly by his own management, Damase had among the gang a number of companions much after his own pattern, and it was clearly his intention to take the lead in the shanty so far as he dared venture. When first he saw Frank, and learned that he was to be with Johnston also, he tried after his own fashion to make friends with him. But as might be expected, neither the man himself nor his overtures of friendship impressed Frank favourably. He wanted neither a pull from his pocket flask nor a chew from his plug of "navy," nor to handle his greasy cards; and although he declined the offer of all these uncongenial things as politely as possible, the veritable suspicious, sensitive, French-Indian nature took offence, which deepened day after day, as he could not help seeing that Frank was careful to give himself and companions as wide a berth as he could without being pointedly rude or offensive.

When one is seeking to gratify evil feelings toward another with whom he has daily contact, the opportunity is apt to be not long in coming, and Damase conceived that he had his chance of venting his spite on Frank by seizing upon the habit of Bible reading and prayer which the lad had as scrupulously observed in the shanty as if he had been at home. As might be imagined, he was altogether alone in this good custom, and at first the very novelty of it had secured him immunity from pointed notice or comment. But when Damase, thinking he saw in his daily devotions an opening for his malicious purposes, drew attention to them by jeering remarks and taunting insinuations, the others, yielding to that natural tendency to be incensed with any one who seems to assert superior goodness, were inclined to side with him, or at all events to make no attempt to interfere.

At first Damase confined himself to making as much noise as possible while Frank was reading his Bible or saying his prayers, keeping up a constant fire of remarks that were aimed directly at the much-tried boy, and which were sometimes clever or impertinent enough to call forth a hearty laugh from his comrades. But finding that Frank was not to be overcome by this, he resorted to more active measures. Pretending to be dancing carelessly about the room he would, as if by accident, bump up against the object of his enmity, sending the precious book flying on the floor, or, if Frank was kneeling by his bunk, tripping and tumbling roughly over his outstretched feet. Another time he knocked the Bible out of his hands with a well-aimed missile, and, again, covered him with a heavy blanket as he knelt at prayer.

All this Frank bore in patient silence, hoping in that way to secure peace in time. But Damase's persecutions showing no signs of ceasing, the poor lad's self-control began to desert him, and at last the crisis came one night when, while he was kneeling as usual at the foot of his bunk, Damase crept up softly behind him, and springing upon his shoulders, brought him sprawling to the floor. In an instant Frank was on his feet, and when the others saw his flashing and indignant countenance and noticed his tight-clinched fists, the roar of laughter that greeted his downfall was checked half way, and a sudden silence fell upon them. They all expected him to fly at his tormentor like a young tiger, and Damase evidently expected it too, for he stepped back a little, and his grinning face sobered as he assumed a defensive attitude.

But Frank had no thought of striking. That was not his way of defending his religion, much as he was willing to endure rather than be unfaithful. Drawing himself up to his full height, and looking a splendid type of righteous indignation, he commanded the attention of all as in clear, strong tones, holding his sturdy fists close to his sides as though he dared not trust them elsewhere, and looking straight into Damase's eyes, he exclaimed,—

"Aren't you ashamed to do such an unmanly thing—you, who are twice my size and age? I have done nothing to you. Why should you torment me? And just when I want most to be quiet, too!"

Then, turning to the other men with a gesture of appeal that was irresistible, he cried,—

"Do you think it's fair, fellows, for that man to plague me so when I've done him no harm? Why don't you stop him? You can do it easy enough. He's nothing but a big coward."

Frank's anger had risen as he spoke, and this last sentence slipped out before he had time to stop it. No sooner was it uttered than he regretted it; but the bolt had been shot, and it went straight to its mark. While Frank had been speaking, Damase was too keen of sight and sense not to notice that the manly speech and fine self-control of the boy were causing a quick revulsion of feeling in his hearers, and that unless diverted they would soon be altogether on his side, and the taunt he had just flung out awoke a deep murmur of applause which was all that was needed to inflame his passion to the highest pitch. The Frenchman looked the very incarnation of fury as, springing towards Frank with uplifted fist, he hissed, rather cried, through his gleaming teeth,—

"Coward! I teach you call me coward."

Stepping back a little, Frank threw up his arms in a posture of defence; for he was not without knowledge of what is so oddly termed "the noble art."

But before the blow fell an unlooked-for intervention relieved him from the danger that threatened.

The foreman, when the shanty was being built, had the farther right-hand corner partitioned off so as to form a sort of cabin just big enough to contain his bunk, his chest, and a small rude table on which lay the books in which he kept his accounts and made memoranda, and some half-dozen volumes that constituted his library. In this nook, shut off from the observation and society of the others, yet able to overhear and, if he chose to open the door, to oversee also all that went on in the larger room, Johnston spent his evenings poring over his books by the light of a tallow candle, the only other light in the room being that given forth by the ever-blazing fire.

Owing to this separation from the others, Johnston had been unaware of the manner in which Frank had been tormented, as it was borne so uncomplainingly. But this time Frank's indignant speech, followed so fast by Damase's angry retort, told him plainly that there was need of his interference. He emerged from his corner just at the moment when Damase was ready to strike. One glance at the state of affairs was enough. Damase's back was turned toward him. With a swift spring, that startled the others as if he had fallen through the roof, he darted forward, and ere the French-Canadian's fist could reach its mark a resistless grasp was laid upon his collar, and, swung clear off his feet, he was flung staggering across the room as though he had been a mere child.

"You Indian dog!" growled Johnston, in his fiercest tones, "what are you about? Don't let me catch you tormenting that boy again!"

CHAPTER VI.

LIFE IN THE LUMBER CAMP.

FOR a moment there was absolute silence in the shanty, the sudden and effectual intervention of the big foreman in Frank Kingston's behalf filling the onlookers with astonishment. But then, as they recovered themselves, there came a burst of laughter that made the rafters ring, in the midst of which Damase, gathering himself together, slunk scowling to his berth with a face that was dark with hate.

Not deigning to take any further notice of him, Johnston turned to go back to his corner, touching Frank on his shoulder as he did so, and saying to him in a low tone,—

"Come with me, my lad; I want a word with you."

Still trembling from the excitement of the scene through which he had just passed, Frank followed the foreman into his little sanctum, the inside of which he had never seen before, for it was kept jealously locked whenever its occupant was absent. Johnston threw himself down on his bunk, and motioned Frank to take a seat upon the chest. For a few moments he regarded him in silence, and so intently that, although his expression was full of kindness, and it seemed of admiration, too, the boy felt his face flushing under his steady scrutiny. At last the foreman spoke.

"You're a plucky lad, Frank. Just like your father—God bless him! He was a good friend to me when I needed a friend sorely. I heard all that went on to-night, though I didn't see it, and had some hint of it before, though I didn't let on, for I wanted to see what stuff you were made of. But you played the man, my boy, and your father would have been proud to see you. Now just you go right ahead, Frank; and if any of those French rascals or anybody else tries to hinder you, out of this shanty he'll go, neck and crop, and stay out, as sure as my name is Dan Johnston."

"You're very kind, Mr. Johnston," said Frank, his eyes glistening somewhat suspiciously, for, to tell the truth, this warm praise coming after the recent strain upon his nerves was a little too much for his self-control. "I felt sometimes like telling you when the men tormented me so; but I didn't want to be a tale-bearer, and I was hoping they'd get tired of it and give up of their own accord."

"It's best as it is, lad," replied Johnston. "If the men found out you told me, they'd be like to think hard of you. But there's no fear of that now. And look here, Frank. After this, when you want to read your Bible in peace, and say your prayers, just come in here. No one'll bother you here, and you can sit down on the chest there and have a quiet time to yourself."

Frank's face fairly beamed with delight at this unexpected invitation, and he stood up on his feet to thank his kind friend.

"Oh, Mr. Johnston, I'm so glad! I've never been able to read my Bible or say my prayers right since I came to the shanty—there's always such a noise going on. But I won't mind that in here. It's so good of you to let me come in."

The foreman smiled in his deep, serious way, and then as he relapsed into silence, and took up again the book he had laid down to spring to Frank's assistance, Frank thought it time to withdraw; and with a respectful "Good-night, sir." which Johnston acknowledged by a nod, returned to the larger room.

The shantymen were evidently awaiting his reappearance with much curiosity; but he went quietly back to his bunk, picked up his Bible, finished the passage in the midst of which he had been interrupted, and, having said his prayers, lay down to sleep without a word to any one; for no one questioned him, and he felt no disposition to start a discussion by questioning any of the others.

From this time forth he could see clearly that two very different opinions concerning himself prevailed in the shanty. By all the English members of the gang, and some of the French, headed by honest Baptiste, he was looked upon, with hearty liking and admiration, as a plucky chap that knew how to take care of himself; by the remainder of the French contingent, with Damase as the ruling spirit, he was regarded as a stuck-up youngster that wanted taking down badly, and who was trying to make himself a special favourite with the foreman, just to advance his own selfish ends. Gladly would Frank have been on friendly terms with all; but this being now impossible, through no fault of his own, he made up his mind to go on his way as quietly as possible, being constantly careful to give no cause of offence to those who, as he well knew, were only too eager to take it.

LIFE IN THE LUMBER CAMP. 73

There were some slight flurries of snow, fragile and short-lived heralds of winter's coming, during the latter part of November, and then December was ushered in by a grand storm that lasted a whole day, and made glad the hearts of the lumbermen by filling the forest aisles with a deep, soft, spotless carpet, that asked only to be packed smooth and hard in order to make perfect roads over which to transport the noble logs that had been accumulating upon the "roll-ways" during the past weeks.

A shantyman is never so completely in his element as when the snow lies two feet deep upon the earth's brown breast. An open winter is his bane, Jack Frost his best friend; and there was a perceptible rise in the spirits of the occupants of Camp Kippewa as the mercury sank lower and lower in the tube of the foreman's thermometer. Plenty of snow meant not only easy hauling all winter long, but a full river and "high water" in the spring-time, and no difficulty in getting the drive of logs that would represent their winter's work down the Kippewa to the Grand River beyond. Frank did not entirely share their exultation. The colder it got the more wood had to be chopped, the more food had to be cooked—for the men's appetites showed a marked increase—and, furthermore, the task of keeping the water-barrels filled became one of serious magnitude. But bracing himself to meet his growing burdens, he toiled away cheerfully, resisting every temptation to grumble, his clear tuneful whistling of the sacred airs in vogue at Calumet making Baptiste, who had a quick ear for music, so familiar with "Rock of Ages," "Abide with Me," "Nearer, my God, to Thee," and other melodies, which have surely strayed down to us from heaven, that unconsciously he took to whistling them himself, much to Frank's amusement and approval.

The days were very much alike. At early dawn, before it was yet light enough to see clearly, Johnston would emerge from his corner, and, in stentorian tones whose meaning was not to be mistaken, shout to the sleeping men scattered along the rows of sloping bunks, "Up with ye, men! up with ye!" And with many a growl and grunt they would, one by one, unroll from their blankets. As their only preparation for bed had been to lay aside their coats and boots or moccasins, the morning toilet did not consume much time. A dash of cold water as an eye-opener, a tugging on of boots or lacing up of moccasins, a scrambling into coats, and that was the sum of it. The only brush and comb in the camp belonged to Frank, and he felt half ashamed to use them, because no one else thought such articles necessary.

Breakfast hurriedly disposed of, all but Baptiste and Frank sallied forth into the snow, to be seen no more until mid-day. There were just fifty persons, all told, in the camp, each man having his definite work to do: the carpenter, whose business it was to keep the sleighs in repair; the teamsters, who directed the hauling of the logs; the "sled-tenders," who saw that the loads were well put on; the "head chopper" and his assistants, whose was the laborious yet fascinating task of felling the forest monarchs; the "sawyers," who cut their prostrate forms into convenient lengths; the "scorers," who stripped off the branches and slab sides from tree trunks set apart for square timber; and finally, the "hewer," who with his huge, broad axe made square the "stick," as the great piece of timber is called.

All these men had to be fed three times a day, and almost insatiable were their appetites, as poor Frank had no chance to forget. Happily they did not demand the same variety in their bill of fare as do the guests at a metropolitan hotel. Pork and beans, bread and tea, these were the staple items. Anything else was regarded as an "extra." A rather monotonous diet, undoubtedly; but it would not be easy to prescribe a better one for men working twelve hours a day, in the open air, through the still, steady cold of a Canadian winter in the backwoods.

At noon the hungry toilers trooped back for dinner, which they devoured in ravenous haste that there might be as much as possible left of the hour for a lounge upon the bunk, with pipe in mouth, in luxurious idleness. Then as the dusk gathered they appeared once more, this time for the night, and disposed to eat their supper with much more decorous slowness. Supper over, the snow-soaked mittens and stockings hung about the fire to dry, and pipes put in full blast, they were ready for song, story, or dance, until bed time.

Thus day followed day, until Frank, whose work kept him closely confined to the camp, grew so weary of it that he was on the verge of heartily repenting that he had ever consented to be a chore-boy, ever thought that was the only condition upon which he could gratify his longing for a lumberman's life, when another mischance became his good fortune, and he was unexpectedly relieved of a large part of his tiresome duties. This was how it came about.

One morning he was surprised by seeing one of the

sleighs returning a good while before the dinner hour, and was somewhat alarmed when he noticed that it bore the form of a man, who had evidently been the victim of an accident. Happily, however, it proved to be not a very serious case. An immense pine in falling headlong had borne with it a number of smaller trees that stood near by, and one of these had fallen upon an unwary "scorer," hurling him to the ground, and badly bruising his right leg, besides causing some internal injury. He was insensible when picked up, but came to himself soon after reaching the shanty, where Frank made him as comfortable as he could, even putting him upon his own mattress that he might lie as easy as possible.

The injured man proved to be one of Damase Deschenaux's allies; but Frank did not let that prevent his showing him every kindness while he was recovering from his injuries, with the result of completely winning the poor ignorant fellow's heart, much to Damase's disgust. Damase, indeed, did his best to persuade Laberge that Frank's attentions were prompted by some secret motive, and that it was not to be trusted. But deeds are far stronger arguments than words, and the sufferer was not to be convinced. By the end of a week he was able to limp about the shanty, but it was very evident that he would not be fit to take up his work again that season. This state of affairs caused the foreman some concern, for he felt loath to send the unfortunate fellow home, and yet he could not keep him in idleness. Then it appeared that what is one man's extremity may be another's opportunity. Johnston knew very well that however bravely he might go about it, Frank's work could not help being distasteful to him, and a bright plan flashed into his mind. Calling Frank into his corner one evening, he said,—

"How would you like, my lad, to have some of the out-door work for a change?"

The mere expression of Frank's face was answer enough. It fairly shone with gladness, as he replied,—

"I would like it above all things, sir, for I am a little tired of being nothing but a chore-boy."

"Well, I think we might manage it, Frank," said the foreman. "You see, Laberge can't do his work again this winter, and it goes against my heart to send him home, for he's nobody but himself to depend upon. So I've hit upon this plan: Laberge can't chop the wood or haul the water, but he can help Baptiste in cooking and cleaning up. Suppose, then,

LIFE IN THE LUMBER CAMP. 79

you were to get the wood ready and see about the water in the morning, and then come out into the woods with us after dinner, leaving Laberge to do the rest of the work. How would that suit you?"

"It would suit me just splendidly, sir," exclaimed Frank, delightedly. "I can see about the wood and water all right before dinner, and I'll be so glad to go to the woods with you. I'll just do the best I can to fill Laberge's place."

"I'm right sure you will, Frank," replied Johnston. "So you may consider it settled for the present, at any rate."

Frank felt like dancing a jig on the way back to his bunk, and not even the scowling face of Damase, who had been listening to the conversation in the foreman's room with keen Indian ears, and had caught enough of it to learn of the arrangement made, could cast any damper upon his spirits. In this case half a loaf was decidedly better than no bread at all. Freedom from the restraints and irksome duties of chore-boy's lot for even half the day was a precious boon, and the happy boy lay down to rest that night feeling like quite a different person from what he had been of late, when there seemed no way of escape from the monotonous, wearisome task he had taken upon himself, except to give it all up and return to Calumet, which was almost the last thing that he could imagine himself doing; for Frank Kingston had plenty of pride as well as pluck, and his love for lumbering had not suffered any eclipse because of his experiences.

But what is one man's meat is another man's poison, according to the homely adage, and in this case what made Frank so happy made Damase miserable. The jealous, revengeful fellow saw in it only another proof of the foreman's favouritism, and was also pleased to regard the relegating of Laberge to the dish-washing and so forth as the degradation of a compatriot, which it behoved him to resent, since Laberge seemed lacking in the spirit to do it himself. Had he imagined that he would meet with the support of the majority, he would have sought to organize a rebellion in the camp. But he knew well enough that such a thing was utterly out of the question, so he was forced to content himself with fresh determinations to "get even" with the foreman and his favourite in some way before the winter passed; and, as will be seen, he came perilously near attaining his object.

CHAPTER VII.

A THRILLING EXPERIENCE.

FRANK was very happy now that the way had been so opportunely opened for him to take part in the whole round of lumbering operations. He awaited with impatience the coming of noon and the rush of hungry men to their hearty dinner, because it was the signal for his release from chore-boy work and promotion to the more honourable position of assistant-teamster. The long afternoons out in the cold, crisp air, amid the thud of well-aimed axes, the crash of falling trees, the shouts of busy men, and all the other noisy incidents of the war they were waging against the innocent, defenceless forest, were precisely what his heart had craved so long, and he felt clearer than ever in his mind that lumbering was the life for him.

After he had been a week at his new employment, Con Murphy, the big teamster to whom he had been assigned by the foreman, with the injunction to "be easy on the lad, and give him plenty of time to get handy," was heard to say in public,—

"Faith, an' he's a broth of a boy, I can tell you; and I wouldn't give him for half-a-dozen of those *parlez-vous* Frenchies—like the chap whose place he took—indade that I wouldn't."

Which, coming to Damase's ears, added further fuel to the fire of jealousy and hate that was burning within this half-savage creature's breast. So fierce indeed were Damase's feelings that he could not keep them concealed, and more than one of the shantymen took occasion to drop a word of warning into Frank's ear about him.

"You'd better keep a sharp eye on that chap Damase, Frank," they would say. "He's an ugly customer, and he seems to have got it in for you."

Frank, on his part, was by no means disposed to laugh at or neglect these kindly warnings. Indeed, he fully intended repeating them to Johnston at the first opportunity. But the days slipped by without a favourable chance presenting itself, and Damase's wild thirst for the revenge which he thought was merited came perilously near a dreadful satisfaction.

February had come, and supplies at the shanty

were running low, so that Foreman Johnston deemed it necessary to pay a visit to the depot to see about having a fresh stock sent out. The first that Frank knew of his intention was the night before he started. He had gone into the foreman's little room as usual to read his Bible and pray, and having finished, was about to slip quietly out, Johnston having apparently been quite unobservant of his presence, when he was asked,—

"How would you like to go over to the depot with me to-morrow?"

How would he like! Such a question to ask of a boy, when it meant a twenty-five miles' drive and a whole day's holiday after months of steady work at the camp!

"I should be delighted, sir," replied Frank, as promptly as he could get the words out.

"Very well, then; you can come along with me. We'll start right after breakfast. Baptiste will have to look after himself for one day," said the foreman. And with a fervent "Thank you, sir," Frank went off, his face wreathed with smiles and his heart throbbing with joy at the prospect before him.

So eager was he that it did not need Johnston's shout of "Turn out, lads, turn out!" to waken him next morning, for he was wide awake already, and he tumbled into his clothes with quite unusual alacrity. So soon as breakfast was over, the foreman had one of the best horses in the stable harnessed to his "jumper," as the low, strong, comfortable wooden sleigh that is alone able to cope with the rough forest roads is called; abundance of thick warm buffalo-robes were provided; and then he and Frank tucked themselves in tightly, and they set out on their long drive to the depot.

The mercury stood at twenty degrees below zero when they started, but they did not mind that. Not a breath of wind stirred the clear cold air. The sun soon rose into the blue vault above them, and shone down upon the vast expanse of snow about them with a vigour that made their eyes blink. The horse was a fine animal, and, having been off duty for a few days previous, was full of speed and spirit, and they glided over the well-beaten portion of the road at a dashing pace. But when they came to the part over which there had been little travel all winter long the going was too heavy for much speed, and often the horse could not do more than walk.

This seemed to Frank just the opportunity for which he had been waiting, to tell the foreman about

A THRILLING EXPERIENCE.

Damase and his threats of revenge. At first Johnston was disposed to make light of the matter, but when Frank told him what he had himself observed, as well as what had been reported to him by the others, the foreman was sufficiently impressed to say,—

"The rascal wants some looking after, that's clear. He's a worthless fellow, anyway, and I'm mighty sorry I ever let him into my gang. I think the best thing will be to drop him as soon as I get back, or he may make some trouble for us. I'm glad you told me this, Frank. I won't forget it."

At the depot they found Alec Stewart, just returned from a tour of inspection of the different camps, and full of hearty welcome. He was very glad to see Frank.

"Ah ha, my boy!" he cried, slapping him vigorously on the back, "I needn't ask you how you are. Your looks answer for you. Why, you must weigh ten pounds more than when I last saw you. Well, what do you think of lumbering now, and how does Mr. Johnston treat you? They tell me," looking at the foreman with a sly smile, "that he's a mighty stiff boss. Is that the way you find him?"

Frank was ready enough to answer all his friend's questions, and to assure him that the foreman treated him like a kind father, and that he himself was fonder of lumbering than ever. Both he and Johnston had famous appetites for the bountiful dinner that was soon spread before them, and the resources of the depot permitting of a much more extensive bill of fare than was possible at the shanty, he felt in duty bound to apologize for the avidity with which he attacked the juicy roast of beef, the pearly potatoes, the toothsome pudding, and the other dainties that, after months of pork and beans, tasted like ambrosia.

The superintendent and the foreman had much to say to one another which did not concern Frank, and so while they talked business he roamed about the place, enjoying the freedom from work, and chatting with the men at the depot, telling them some of his experiences and being told some of their in return. Happening to mention Damase Deschenaux, one of the men at once exclaimed,—

"That's a first-class scoundrel! It beats me to understand why Johnston has him in his gang. He's sure to raise trouble wherever he goes."

Frank felt tempted to tell how Damase had "raised trouble" with him, but thought he would better not, and the talk soon turned in another direction.

The afternoon was waning before Johnston prepared to start on the return journey, and Mr. Stewart tried hard to persuade him to stay for the night— an invitation that Frank devoutly hoped would be accepted. But the big foreman would not hear of it.

"No, no," said he in his decided way, "I must get back to the shanty. There's been only half a day's work done to-day, I'll warrant you, because I wasn't on hand to keep the beggars at it. Why, they'll lie abed till mid-day to-morrow if I'm not there to rouse them out of their bunks."

Whatever Johnston said he stuck to, so there was no use in argument, and shortly after four o'clock he and Frank tucked themselves snugly into the jumper again and drove away from the depot, Stewart shouting after them,—

"If you change your mind after you've gone a couple of miles, don't feel delicate about coming back. I won't laugh at you."

Johnston's only answer was a grim smile and a crack of the whip over the horse's hind-quarters that sent him off at full gallop, the snow flying in clouds from his plunging feet into the faces of his passengers.

The hours crept by as the sleigh made its slow way over the heavy ground, and Frank, as might be expected after the big dinner he had eaten, began to feel very sleepy. There was no reason why he should not yield to the seductive influence of the drowsy god, so, sinking down low into the seat and drawing the buffalo-robe up over his head, he soon was lost to sight and sense. While he slept the night fell, and they were still many miles from home. The cold was great, but not a breath of wind stirred the intense stillness. The stars shone out like flashing diamonds set in lapis-lazuli. Silence reigned supreme, save as it was intruded upon by the heavy breathing of the frost-flaked horse and the crunching of the runners through the crisp snow.

Johnston felt glad when they breasted the hill on the other side of which was Deep Gully, crossed by a rude corduroy bridge; for that bridge was just five miles from the camp, and another hour, at the farthest, would bring them to the end of their journey.

When the top of the hill was reached, the foreman gathered up the reins, called upon the horse to quicken his pace, and away they went down the slope at a tearing gallop.

Deep Gully well deserved the name that had been given it when the road was made. A turbulent torrent among the hills had in the course of time eaten a

A THRILLING EXPERIENCE.

way for itself, which, although very narrow, made up for its lack of breadth by a great degree of depth. It was a rather picturesque place in summer time, when abundant foliage softened its steep sides; but in winter, when it seemed more like a crevasse in a glacier than anything else, there was no charm about it. The bridge that crossed it was a very simple affair, consisting merely of two long stringers laid six feet apart, and covered with flattened timbers.

Upon this slight structure the jumper descended with a bump that woke Frank from his pleasant nap, and, putting aside the buffalo-robe, he sat up in the sleigh to gather his wits. It was well he did, for if ever he needed them it was at that moment. Almost simultaneous with the thud of the horse's feet upon the bridge there came a crash, a sound of rending timbers, the bridge quivered like a ship struck by a mighty billow, and the next instant dropped into the chasm below, bearing with it a man, and boy, and horse, and sleigh!

Full thirty feet they fell; the bridge, which had given way at one end only, hurling them from it so that they landed at the bottom of Deep Gully in a confused heap, yet happily free from entanglement with its timbers. So soon as he felt himself falling

Frank threw aside the robes and made ready to spring; but Johnston instinctively held on to the reins, with the result that, being suddenly dragged forward by the frantic plunging of the terrified animal, he received a kick in the forehead that rendered him insensible, and would have dashed his brains out but for the thick fur cap he wore, while the jumper, turning over upon him, wrenched his leg so as to render him completely helpless.

Frank was more fortunate. His timely spring, aided by the impetus of their descent, carried him clear of the horse and sleigh, and sent him headlong into a deep drift that filled a hollow at the gully's bottom. The snow-bank opened its arms to receive him, and buried him to the hips. The first shock completely deprived him of breath, and almost of his senses too. But beyond that he received no injury, and was soon struggling with all his might to free himself from the snow that held him captive. This proved to be no easy task. He was pretty firmly embedded, and at first it seemed as though his efforts at release only made his position worse.

"This is a fine fix to be in!" said he to himself. "Buried in a snow-drift; and dear knows what's happened to Mr. Johnston."

He had been hoping that the foreman would come to his assistance, but getting no reply to his shouts, he began to fear lest his companion might be unable to render any help. Perhaps, indeed, he might be dead! The thought roused him to still greater exertions, and at last by a heroic effort he succeeded in turning a kind of somersault in his cold prison, which had the happy result of putting his head where his heels had been. To scramble out altogether was then an easy job, and in another instant he was beside the sleigh.

His first thought was that his worst fears were realized. Certainly the sight was one that might have filled a stouter heart with chill alarm. The horse had fallen into a deep drift, which covered him to the shoulders, and rendered him utterly helpless, entangled as he was with the harness and the overturned jumper. He had evidently, like Frank, been struggling violently to free himself, but finding it useless, had for a time ceased his efforts, and stood wild-eyed and panting, the picture of animal terror. On seeing Frank he made another frantic plunge or two, looking at the boy with an expression of agonized appeal, as though he would say,—

"Oh, help me out of this dreadful place!"

And glad would Frank have been to respond to the best of his ability. But the poor horse could not be considered first. Half under the sleigh, half buried in the snow, lay the big foreman, to all appearance dead, the blood flowing freely from an ugly gash in his forehead, where the fur cap had failed to protect him entirely from the horse's hoof.

Frank sprang to his side, and with a tremendous effort turned him over upon his back, and getting out his handkerchief, wiped the blood away from his face. As he did so, the first awful thought of death gave way to a feeling of hope. White and still as Johnston lay, his face was warm, and he was surely breathing a little. Seizing a handful of snow, Frank pressed it to the foreman's forehead, and cried to him as though he were asleep,—

"Mr. Johnston, Mr. Johnston! What's the matter with you? Tell me, won't you?"

For some minutes there was no sign of response. Then the injured man stirred, gave a deep sigh followed by a groan, opened his eyes with a look of dazed bewilderment, and put his hand up to his head, which was evidently giving him intense pain.

"Oh, Mr. Johnston, I'm so glad! I was afraid you

were dead!" exclaimed Frank. "Can't I help you to get up?"

Turning upon his shoulder, the foreman made an effort to raise himself, but at once sank back with a groan.

"I'm sore hurt, my lad," he said; "I can't stir. You'll have to get help."

And so great was his suffering that he well nigh lost consciousness again.

Frank tried his best to lift him away from the sleigh, but found the task altogether beyond his young strength in that deep snow, and had to give it up as hopeless. Certainly he was in a most trying situation for a mere boy—fully five miles from the shanty, with an almost untravelled road between that must be traversed by him alone, while the injured man would have to lie helpless in the snow until his return. Little wonder if he felt in sore perplexity as to what should be done, and how he should act under the circumstances.

CHAPTER VIII.

IN THE NICK OF TIME.

IF Frank was undecided, Mr. Johnston's mind was fully made up.

"Our only chance is for you to get to the shanty at once, Frank. It'll be a hard job, my boy, but you'll have to try it," said he.

"But what'll become of you, sir, staying here all alone? The wolves might find you out, and how could you defend yourself then?" asked Frank, in sore bewilderment as to the solution of the dilemma.

"I'll have to take my chances of that, Frank; for if I stay here all night, I'll freeze to death, anyway. So just throw the buffaloes over me, and put for the shanty as fast as you can," replied the foreman.

Unable to suggest any better plan, Frank covered Johnston carefully with the robes, making him as comfortable as he could; then buttoning up his coat and pulling his cap on tightly, he was about to scramble up the steep side of the gully to regain the road, when the foreman said, in a low tone, almost a whisper,—

"This is about the time you generally say your prayers, Frank. Couldn't you say them here before you start?"

With quick intuition Frank divined the big bashful man's meaning. It was his roundabout way of asking the boy to commit him to the care of God before leaving him alone in his helplessness.

Feeling half condemned at not having thought of it himself, Frank came back, and kneeling close beside his friend, lifted up his voice in prayer with a fervour and simplicity that showed how strong and sure was his faith in the love and power of his Father in heaven. When he had finished his petition, the foreman added to it an "Amen" that seemed to come from the very depths of his heart; and then yielding to an impulse that was irresistible, Frank bent down and implanted a sudden kiss upon the pale face looking at him with such earnest, anxious eyes. This unexpected proof of warm affection completely overcame the foreman, whose feelings had been already deeply stirred by the prayer. Strong, reserved man as he was, he could not keep back the tears.

"God bless you, my boy!" he murmured huskily. "If I get safely out of this, I shall be a different man. You have taught me a lesson I won't forget."

"God bless you and take care of you, sir!" answered Frank. "I hope nothing will happen to you while I'm away, and I'll be back as soon as I can."

The next moment he was making his way up the gully's side, and soon a triumphant shout announced that he had reached the road and was off for the lumber camp at his best speed.

The task before him was one from which many a grown man might have shrunk in dismay. For five long, lonely miles the road ran through the forest that darkened it with heavy shadows, and not a living soul could he hope to meet until he reached the shanty.

It was now past eight o'clock, and to do his best it would take him a whole hour to reach his goal. The snow lay deep upon the road, and was but little beaten down by the few sleighs that had passed over it. The air was keen and crisp with frost, the temperature being many degrees below zero. And finally, the most fear-inspiring of all, there was the possibility of wolves: for the dreaded timber wolf had been both heard and seen in close proximity to the camp of late, an unusual scarcity of small game having made him daring in his search for food.

But Frank possessed a double source of strength. He was valiant by nature, and he had implicit faith in God's overruling providence. He felt specially under the divine care now, and resolutely putting away all thoughts of personal danger, addressed himself, mind and body, to the one thing—the relief of Johnston from his perilous position.

With arms braced at his sides and head bent forward, he set out at a jog-trot, which was better suited for getting through the deep snow than an ordinary walk. Fortunately he was in the very pink of condition. The steady, hard work of the preceding months, combined with the coarse but abundant food and early hours, had developed and strengthened every muscle in his body and hardened his constitution until few boys of his age could have been found better fitted to endure a long tramp through heavy snow than he. Moreover, running had always been his favourite form of athletic exercise, and the muscles it required were well trained for their work.

"I'll do it all right inside the hour," he said to himself. And then, as a sudden thought struck him, he gave a nervous little laugh, and added, "And perhaps make a good deal better time if I hear anything of the wolves."

Try as he might, he could not get the wolves out of his head. He had not himself seen any signs of them, but several times the choppers working farthest from the camp had mentioned finding their tracks in the snow, and once they had been heard howling in the distance after the men had all come into the shanty for the night.

On he went through the snow and night, now making good progress at his brisk jog-trot, now going more slowly as he dropped into a walk to rest himself and recover breath. Although the moon rode high in the heavens, the trees which stood close to the road allowed few of her beams to light his path.

"If it was only broad daylight I wouldn't mind it a bit," Frank soliloquized; "but this going alone at this time of night is not the sort of a job I care for."

And then the thought of poor Johnston lying helpless but uncomplaining in the snow made him feel ashamed of his words, and to ease his conscience he broke into a trot again. Just as he did so a sound reached his ear that sent a thrill of terror to his heart. Hoping he might be mistaken, he stopped and listened with straining senses. For a moment

## IN THE NICK OF TIME.	99

there was absolute silence. Then the sound came again—distant, but clear and unmistakable. He had heard it only once before, yet he felt as sure of it now as if it had been his mother's voice. It was the howl of the timber wolf sounding through the still night air from somewhere to the north; how far away he could not determine.

At the sound all his strength seemed to leave him. How helpless he was alone in that mighty forest without even so much as a knife wherewith to defend himself! But it would not do to stand irresolute. His own life as well as the foreman's depended upon his reaching the shanty. Were he to climb one of the big trees that stood around, the wolves, of course, could not get at him; but Johnston would be dead before daylight came to release him from his tree citadel, and perhaps he would himself fall a victim to the cold in that exposed situation. There was no other alternative than to run for his life, so, breathing out a fervent prayer for divine help and protection, he summoned all his energies to the struggle. He was more than a mile from the shanty, and his exertion had told severely upon his strength; but the great peril of his situation made him forget his weariness, and he started off as if he were perfectly fresh.

But the howling of the wolves grew more and more distinct as they drew swiftly nearer, and with agony of heart the poor boy felt his breath coming short and his limbs beginning to fail beneath him. Nearer and nearer came his dreaded pursuers, and every moment he expected to see them burst into the road behind him.

Fortunately, he had reached a part of the road which, being near the camp, was much used by the teams drawing logs to the river-bank, and was consequently beaten hard and smooth. This welcome change enabled him to quicken his steps, which had dropped into a walk; and although he felt almost blind from exhaustion, he pushed desperately forward, hoping at every turn of the road to catch a glimpse of the shanty showing dark through the trees. The cry of the disciples caught in the sudden storm on Galilee, "Lord, save us; we perish!" kept coming to his lips as he staggered onward. Surely there could not be much further to go! He turned for a moment to look behind him. The wolves were in sight, their dark forms showing distinctly against the snow as in silence now they gained upon their prey. Run as hard as he might, they must be upon him ere another fifty yards were passed. He felt as

IN THE NICK OF TIME. 101

if it were all over with him, and so utter was his exhaustion that it seemed to benumb his faculties and make him half willing for the end to come.

But the end was not to be as the wolves desired. Just at the critical moment, when further exertion seemed impossible, he caught sight of some one approaching him rapidly from the direction of the shanty, and shouting aloud while he rushed forward to meet him. With one last supreme effort he plunged toward this timely apparition, and a moment later fell insensible at his feet.

It was Baptiste—good-hearted, affectionate Baptiste—who, having awaited the travellers' return and grown concerned at their long delay, had gone out to look along the road to see if they were anywhere in view. Catching sight of Frank's lonely figure, he had made all haste to meet him, and reached him just in time to ward off the wolves that in a minute more would have been upon him.

When the wolves saw Baptiste, who swung a gleaming axe about his head, as he shouted, "*Chiens donc!* I'll split your heads eef I get at you!" they stopped short, and even retreated a little, drawing themselves together in a sort of group in the middle of the road, snapping their teeth and snarling in a half-frightened, half-furious manner. But Baptiste was not to be daunted. Lifting his axe on high, he shouted at them in his choicest French, and charged upon the pack as though they had been simply a flock of marauding sheep. Wolves are arrant cowards, and without pausing to take into consideration the disparity of numbers, for they stood twelve to one, they fled ignominiously before the plucky Frenchman, not halting until they had put fifty yards between themselves and him. Whereupon Baptiste seized upon the opportunity to pick up the still senseless Frank, throw him over his broad shoulder, and hasten back to the shanty before the wolves should regain their self-possession.

They were all asleep in the shanty when the cook returned with his unconscious burden; but he soon roused the others with his vigorous shouts, and by the time they were fully awake, Frank was awake too, the warm air of the room quickly reviving him from his faint. Looking round about with a bewildered expression, he asked anxiously,—

"Where is Mr. Johnston? Hasn't he come back too?"

Then he recollected himself, and a picture of his good friend lying prostrate and helpless in the snow,

IN THE NICK OF TIME. 103

perhaps surrounded by the same wolves that brave Baptiste had rescued him from, flashed into his mind, and springing to his feet he cried,—

"Hurry—hurry! Mr. Johnston is in Deep Gully, and he can't move. The bridge broke under us, and he was almost killed. Oh, hurry, won't you, or the wolves will be after him!"

The men looked at one another in astonishment and horror.

"Deep Gully!" they exclaimed. "That's five miles off. We must go at once."

And immediately all was bustle and excitement as they prepared to go out into the night. As lumbermen always sleep in their clothes, they did not take long to dress, and in a wonderfully short space of time the teamsters had a sleigh with a pair of horses at the door, upon which eight of the men, armed with guns and axes, sprang, and off they went along the road as fast as the horses could gallop. Frank wanted to accompany them, but Baptiste would not allow him.

"No, no, *mon cher*. You must stay wid me. You tired out. They get him all right, and bring him safe home."

And he was fain to lie back, so tortured with

anxiety for the foreman that he could hardly appreciate the blessing of rest, although his own exertions had been tremendous.

Not sparing the horses, the rescuers sped over the road, ever now and then discharging a gun, in order to let Johnston know of their approach and keep his courage up. In less than half-an-hour they reached the gully, and peering over the brink, beheld the dark heap in the snow below that was the object of their search. One glance was sufficient to show how timely was their coming, for almost encircling the hapless man were smaller shapes that even at that distance could be readily recognized.

"We're too late!" cried one of the men; "they're wolves." And with a wild shout he flung himself recklessly down the snowy slope, and others followed close behind.

Before their tumultuous onset the wolves fled like leaves before the autumn wind, and poor Johnston, almost dead with pain, cold, and exhaustion, raising himself a little from the snow, called out in a faint but joyful tone,—

"Thank God, you've come in time! I thought it was all over with me."

CHAPTER IX.

OUT OF CLOUDS, SUNSHINE.

GREAT was the joy of the men at finding Johnston alive and still able to speak, and at once their united strength was applied to extricating him from his painful position. The poor horse, utterly unable to help himself, had long ago given up the vain struggle, and in a state of pitiful exhaustion and fright was lying where he first fell, the snow all about him being torn up in a way that showed how furious had been his struggles. Johnston had by dint of heroic exertion managed to withdraw his leg a little from underneath the heavy jumper; but he could not free himself altogether, so that had the wolves found out how completely both horse and man were in their power, they would have made short work of both. Fortunately, by vigorous shouting and wild waving of his arms, the foreman had been able to keep the cowardly creatures at bay long enough to allow the rescuing party to reach him. But he could not have kept up many minutes more, and if strength and voice had entirely forsaken him the dreadful end would soon have followed.

Handling the injured man with a tenderness and care one would hardly have looked for in such rough fellows, the lumbermen after no small exertion got him up out of the gully and laid him upon the sleigh in the road. Then the horse was released from the jumper, and, being coaxed to his feet, led down the gully to where the sides were not so steep and he could scramble up, while the jumper itself was left behind to be recovered when they had more time to spare.

Before they started off for the shanty one of the men had the curiosity to cross the gully and examine the bridge where it broke, in order to find out the cause of the accident. When he returned there was a strange expression on his face, which added to the curiosity of the others who were awaiting his report.

"Both stringers are sawed near through!" he exclaimed. "And it's not been done long, either. Must have been done to-day, for the sawdust's lying round still."

The men looked at one another in amazement and

horror. The stringers sawed through! What scoundrel could have done such a thing? Who was the murderous traitor in their camp? Then to the quickest-witted of them came the thought of Damase's dire threat and consuming jealousy.

"I know who did it," he cried. "There's only one man in the camp villain enough to do it. It was that hound Damase, as sure as I stand here!"

Instantly the others saw the matter in the same light. Damase had done it beyond a doubt, hoping thereby to have the revenge for which his savage heart thirsted. Ill would it have gone with him could the men have laid hands on him at that moment. They were just in the mood to have inflicted such punishment as would probably have put the wretch in a worse plight than his intended victim, and many and fervent were their vows of vengeance, expressed in language rather the reverse of polite. Strict almost to severity as Johnston was in his management of the camp, the majority of the men, including all the best elements, regarded him with deep respect, if not affection; and that Damase Deschenaux should make so dastardly an attempt upon his life aroused in them a storm of indignant wrath which would not soon be allayed.

They succeeded in making the sufferer quite comfortable upon the sleigh; but they had to go very slowly on the return journey to the shanty, both to make it easy for Johnston, and because the men had to walk now that the sleigh was occupied. So soon as they came in sight, Frank ran to meet them, calling out eagerly,—

"Is he all right? Have you got him?"

"We've got him, Frank, safe enough," replied the driver of the sleigh. "But we wasn't a minute too soon, I can tell you. I guess you must have sent your wolves off to him when you'd done with them."

"Were the wolves at you, sir?" exclaimed Frank, bending over the foreman, and looking anxiously into his face.

Johnston had fallen into a sort of doze or stupor; but the stopping of the sleigh and Frank's anxious voice aroused him, and he opened his eyes with a smile that told plainly how dear to him the boy had become.

"They weren't quite at me, Frank, but they soon would have been if the men hadn't come along," he replied.

With exceeding tenderness the big helpless man was lifted from the sleigh and placed in his own bunk in the corner. The whole shanty was awake to receive him, a glorious fire roared and crackled upon the hearth, and the pleasant fragrance of fresh-brewed tea filled the room. So soon as the foreman's outer garments had been removed, Frank brought him a pannikin of the lumberman's pet beverage, and he drank it eagerly, saying that it was all the medicine he needed. Beyond making him as comfortable as possible, nothing further could be done for him, and in a little while the shantymen were all asleep again as soundly as though there had been no disturbance of their slumbers. Frank wanted to sit up with Johnston; but the foreman would not hear of it, and, anyway, thoroughly sincere as was his offer, he never could have carried it out, for he was very weary himself and ready to drop asleep at the first chance.

Of Damase there was no sign. Some of the men had noticed him quitting work earlier than usual in the afternoon, and when he did not appear at supper-time had thought he was gone off hunting, which he loved to do whenever he got the opportunity. Whether or not he would have the assurance to return to the shanty would depend upon whether he had waited in ambush to see the result of his villany; for if he had done so, and had witnessed the at least partial failure of his plot, there was little chance of his being seen again.

The next morning a careful examination of Johnston showed that, while no bones were broken, his right leg had been very badly twisted and strained almost to dislocation, and he had been internally injured to an extent that could be determined only by a doctor. It was decided to send a message for the nearest doctor, and meanwhile to do everything possible for the sufferer in the way of bandages and liniments that the simple shanty outfit afforded. By general understanding Frank assumed the duties of nurse; and it was not long before life at the camp settled down into its accustomed routine, Johnston having appointed the most experienced and reliable of the gang its foreman during his confinement. In due time the doctor came, examined his patient, made everybody glad by announcing that none of the injuries were serious, and that they required only time and attention for their cure, wrote out full directions for Frank to follow, and then, congratulating Johnston upon his good fortune in having so devoted and intelligent a nurse, set off again on the long drive to his distant home with the pleasant consciousness of having done his duty and earned a good fee.

The weeks that followed were the happiest Frank spent that winter. His duties as nurse were not onerous, and he enjoyed very much the importance with which they invested him. So long as his patient was well looked after, he was free to come and go according to his inclinations, and the thoughtful foreman saw to it that he spent at least half the day in the open air, often sending him with messages to the men working far off in the woods. Frank always carried his rifle with him on these tramps, and frequently brought back with him a brace of hares or partridges, which, having had the benefit of Baptiste's skill, were greatly relished by Johnston, who found his appetite for the plain fare of the shanty much dulled by his confinement.

As the days slipped by the foreman began to open his heart to his young companion and to tell him much about his boyhood, which deeply interested Frank. Living a frontier life, he had his full share of adventure in hunting, lumbering, and prospecting for limits, and many an hour was spent reviewing the past. One evening while they were thus talking together, Johnston became silent and fell into a sort of reverie, from which he presently roused himself, and looking very earnestly into Frank's face, asked him,—

"Have you always been a Christian, Frank?"

The question came so unexpectedly and was so direct that Frank was quite taken aback, and being slow to answer, the foreman, as if fearing he had been too abrupt, went on to say,—

"The reason I asked was because you seem to enjoy so much reading your Bible and saying your prayers that I thought you must have had those good habits a long time."

Frank had now fully recovered himself, and with a blush that greatly became him, answered modestly,—

"I have always loved God. Mother taught me how good and kind he is as soon as I was old enough to understand; and the older I get the more I want to love him and to try to do what is right."

A look of ineffable tenderness came into Johnston's dark eyes while the boy was speaking. Then his face darkened, and giving vent to a heavy sigh, he passed his hand over his eyes as though to put away some painful recollection. After a moment's silence, he said,—

"My mother loved her Bible, and wanted me to love it too. But I was a wild, headstrong chap, and didn't take kindly to the notion of being religious, and I'm afraid I cost her many a tear. God bless her! I wonder does she ever up there think of her son down here, and wonder if he's any better than he was when she had to leave him to look after himself."

Not knowing just what to say, Frank made no reply, but his face glowed with sympathetic interest; and after another pause the foreman went on,—

"I've been thinking a great deal lately, Frank, and it's been all your doing. Seeing you so particular about your religion, and not letting anything stop you from saying your prayers and reading your Bible just as you would at home, has made me feel dreadfully ashamed of myself, and I've been wanting to have a talk with you about it. Would you mind reading your Bible to me? I haven't been inside a church for many a year, and I guess I'd be none the worse of a little Bible-reading."

Frank could not restrain an exclamation of delight. Would he mind? Had not this very thing been on his conscience for weeks past? Had he not been hoping and praying for a good opportunity to propose it himself, and only kept back because of his fear lest the foreman should think this offer presumptuous?

"I shall be very glad indeed to read my Bible to

you, sir," he answered eagerly. "I've been wanting to ask if I mightn't do it, but was afraid that perhaps you would not like it."

"Well, Frank, to be honest with you, I'd a good deal rather have you read to me than read it for myself," said Johnston; "because you must know it 'most by heart, and I've forgotten what little I did know once."

The reading began that night, and thenceforward was never missed while the two were at Camp Kippewa. Young as Frank was, he had learned from his parents and at the Sunday school a great deal about the Book of books, and especially about the life of Christ, so that to Johnston he seemed almost a marvel of knowledge. It was beautiful to see the big man's simplicity as he sat at the feet, so to speak, of a mere boy, and learned anew from him the sublime and precious gospel truths that the indifference and neglect of more than forty years had buried in dim obscurity; and Frank found an ever-increasing pleasure in repeating the comments and explanations that he had heard from the dear lips at home. Even to his young eyes it was clear that the foreman was thoroughly in earnest, and would not stop short of a full surrender of himself to the Master he had so long refused to acknowledge. Above all things, he was a thorough man, and therefore this would take time, for he would insist upon knowing every step of the way; but once well started, no power on earth or beneath would be permitted to bar his progress to the very end.

And this great end was achieved before he left his bunk to resume his work. He lay down there bruised and crippled and godless; but he arose healed and strengthened and a new man in Christ Jesus! If Frank was proud of his big convert, who can blame him? But for his coming to the camp, Johnston might have remained as he was, caring for none of those things which touched his eternal interests; but now through the influence of his example, aided by favouring circumstances, he had been led to the Master's feet.

But Damase—what of Damase? There is not much to tell. Whether or not he was watching when the bridge fell, and how he spent that night, no one ever knew. The next morning he was seen at the depot, where he explained his presence by saying that the foreman had "bounced" him, and that he was going back to his native town. Beyond this, nothing further was ever heard of him.

CHAPTER X.

A HUNTING-TRIP.

THE hold of winter had begun to relax ere Johnston was able fully to resume his work, and a good deal of time having been lost through his accident, every effort had to be exerted to make it up ere the warm sunshine should put an end to the winter's work. Frank was looking forward eagerly to the day when they should break camp, for, to tell the truth, he felt that he had had quite enough of it for one season, and he was longing to be back in Calumet and enjoying the comforts of home once more. He was not exactly homesick. You would have very much offended him by hinting at that. He was simply tired of the monotony of camp fare and camp life, and anxious to return to civilization. So he counted the days that must pass before the order to break camp would come, and felt very light of heart when the sun shone warm, and correspondingly downcast when the thermometer sank below zero, as it was still liable to do.

"Striving" was the order of the day at the lumber camp—that is, the different gangs of choppers and sawyers and teamsters vied with each other as to which could chop, saw, and haul the most logs in a day. The amount of work they could accomplish when thus striving might astonish Mr. Gladstone himself, from eighty to one hundred logs felled and trimmed being the day's work of two men. Frank was deeply interested in this competition, and enjoying the fullest confidence of the men, he was unanimously appointed scorer, keeping each gang's "tally" in a book, and reporting the results to the foreman, who heartily encouraged the rivalry among his men; for the harder they worked the better would be the showing for the season, and he was anxious not to lose the reputation he had won of turning out more logs at his shanty than did any other foreman on the Kippewa.

As the weeks passed and March gave way to April, and April drew toward its close, the lumbermen's work grew more and more arduous; but they kept at it bravely until at last, near the end of April, the snow became so soft in the woods and the roads so bad that no more hauling could be done, and the whole attention of the camp was then given to getting the logs that had been gathering at the river-side all through the winter out upon the ice, so that they might be sure to be carried off by the spring floods. This work did not require all hands, and Johnston now saw the way clear to giving Frank a treat that he had long had in mind for him, but had said nothing about. They were having their usual chat together before going to bed, when the foreman said,—

"Is there anything you would like to do before we break up camp?"

Frank did not at first see the drift of the question, and looking at Johnston with a puzzled sort of expression, replied, questioningly,—

"I don't know. I've had a very good time here."

"Well, but can you think of anything you would like to do before you go back to Calumet?" persisted the foreman. "I'm asking you because there'll not be enough work to go round next week, and you can have a bit of holiday. Now, isn't there something you would like to have a taste of while you have the chance?" And as he spoke his eyes were directed toward the wall at the head of his bed, where hung his rifle, powder-flask, and hunting knife. Frank caught his meaning at once.

"Oh, I see what you are driving at now!" he exclaimed. "You want to know if I wouldn't like to go out hunting."

"Right you are," said Johnston. "Would you?"

"Would I?" cried Frank. "Would a duck swim? Just try me, that's all."

"Well, I do intend to try you," returned Johnston. "The firm have some limits over there near the foot of the mountain that they want me to prospect before I go back, and pick out the best place for a camp. I've been trying to make out to go over there all winter, but getting hurt upset my plans, and I've not had a chance until now. So I'm thinking of making a start to-morrow. There's nothing much else to do except to finish getting the logs on the ice, and I can trust the men to see to that; and, no odds what kind of weather we have, the ice can't start for a week at least. So if you'd like to come along with me and take your rifle, you may get a chance to have a shot at something before we get back. Does that suit you?"

This proposition suited Frank admirably. A week in the woods in Johnston's company could not fail to be a week of delight, and he thanked the foreman in his warmest words for offering to take him on his prospecting tour.

The following morning they set off, the party consisting of four—namely, the foreman, Frank, Laberge, who accompanied them as cook, and another man named Booth as a sort of assistant. The snow still lay deep enough to render snow-shoes necessary, and while Johnston and Frank carried their rifles, Laberge and Booth drew behind them a toboggan, upon which was packed a small tent and an abundant supply of provisions. Their route led straight into the heart of the vast and so far little-explored forest, and away from the river beside whose bank they had been living all winter. It was Johnston's purpose to penetrate to the foot of the mountain range that rose into sight nearly thirty miles away, and then work backward by a different route, noting carefully the lie of the land, the course of the streams, and the best bunches of timber, so as to make sure of selecting a site for the future camp in the very best locality.

He was evidently in excellent spirits himself at the prospect of a week's holiday, for such it would really be, and all trace of his injury having entirely disappeared, there was no drawback to the energy with

A HUNTING-TRIP. 121

which he led his little expedition into the forest where they would be buried for the rest of the week.

The weather was as fine as heart could wish. All day the sun shone brightly, and even at night the temperature never got anywhere near zero, so that with a buffalo-robe under you and a couple of good blankets over you it was possible to sleep quite comfortably in a canvas tent.

"I can't promise you much in the way of game, Frank," said Johnston, as the two tramped along side by side. "It is too late in the season. But the bears must be out of their dens by this time, and if we see one we'll do our best to get his skin for you to take home."

The idea of bringing a big bear-skin home as a trophy of his first real hunting expedition pleased Frank mightily, and his eyes flashed as he grasped his rifle in a way that would in itself have been sufficient warning to bruin, could he only have seen it, to keep well out of the way of so doughty an assailant.

"I'd like immensely to have a shot at a bear, sir," he replied. "So I do hope we shall see one."

"You must be precious careful, though, Frank," said Johnston, "for they're generally in mighty bad humour at this time of year, and you need to get your work in quick, or they may make short work of you."

Various kinds of game were seen during the next day or two, and Frank had many a shot. But Johnston seldom fired, preferring to let Frank have all the fun, as he said. One afternoon, just before they went into camp, the keen eyes of Laberge detected something among the branches of a pine a little distance to the right of their path which caused his face to glow with excitement as he pointed eagerly to it, and exclaimed,—

"*Voila!* A lucifee—shoot him, quick!"

They all turned in the direction he pointed out, and there, sure enough, was a dark mass in the fork of the tree that, as they hastened toward it, resolved itself into a fierce-looking creature, full four times the size of an ordinary cat, which, instead of showing any fear at their approach, bristled up its back and uttered a deep, angry snarl that spoke volumes for its courage.

"Now, then, Frank," said Johnston, "take first shot, and see if you can fetch the brute down."

Trembling with excitement, Frank threw up his rifle, did his best to steady himself, took aim at the bewhiskered muzzle of the lynx, and pulled the trigger. The sharp crack of the rifle was followed by an ear-piercing shriek of mingled pain and rage, and the next instant the wounded creature launched forth into the air toward the hunters. Frank's nervousness, natural enough under the circumstances, had caused him to miss his mark a little, and the bullet, instead of piercing the " lucifee's " brain, had only stung him sorely in the shoulder.

But quick as was its movements, Johnston was still quicker, and the moment its feet touched the snow, ere it could gather itself for another spring, his rifle cracked and a bullet put an end to its career.

"Just as well you weren't by yourself, Frank; hey?" said he, with a smile of satisfaction at the accuracy of his shot. "This chap would have been an ugly customer at close quarters, and," turning the body over to find where the first bullet had hit, "you see you hardly winged him."

Frank blushed furiously and looked very much ashamed of himself for not being a better marksman; but the foreman cheered him up by assuring him that he had really done very well in hitting the animal at all at that distance.

"You only want a little practice, my boy," said he.

"You have plenty of pluck; there's no mistake about that."

The lynx had a fine skin, which Laberge deftly removed, and it was given to Frank because he had fired the first shot at it, so that he would not go back to Calumet without at least one hunting trophy on the strength of which he might do a little boasting.

Further and further into the forest the little party pierced their way, not following any direct line, but making detours to right and left, in order that the country might be thoroughly inspected. As they neared the mountains the trees diminished in size and the streams shrank until, at the end of their journey, the first were too small to pay for cutting, and the second too shallow to be any good for floating. With no little difficulty they ascended a shoulder of the mountain range, in order to get a look over all the adjoining country, and then, Johnston having made up his mind as to the location of the best bunches of timber and the most convenient site for the projected lumber camp, the object of the expedition was accomplished, and they were at liberty to return to the shanty. But before they could do this they were destined to have an adventure that came perilously near taking away from them the youngest of their number.

It was the afternoon before they struck camp on the return journey. The foreman was sitting by the tent mending one of his snow-shoes, which had been damaged tramping through the bush, Booth was busy cutting firewood, and Laberge making preparations for the evening meal. Having nothing else to do, Frank picked up his rifle and sauntered off toward the mountain side, with no very clear idea as to anything more than to kill a little time. Whistling cheerfully one of the many sacred melodies he knew and loved, he made his way over the snow, being soon lost to sight from the camp, Johnston calling after him just before he disappeared,—

"Take care of yourself, my boy, and don't go too far."

To which Frank responded with a smiling, "All right, sir."

At the distance of about a quarter of a mile from the camp he noticed a sort of rift in the mountain, where the rocks were bare and exposed, and at the end of this rift a dark aperture was visible, which at once attracted his attention.

The boy that could come across a cave without

being filled with a burning curiosity to take a peep in and, if possible, explore its interior, would have to be a very dull fellow, and Frank certainly was not of that kind. This dark aperture was no doubt the mouth of a cave of some sort, and he determined to inspect it. When he got within about fifteen yards, he noticed what he had not seen before, that there was a well-defined track leading from the cave to the underbrush to the right, which had evidently been made by some large animal; and with somewhat of a start Frank immediately thought of a bear.

Now, of course, under the circumstances, there was but one thing for him to do if he wished to illustrate his common sense, and that was to hurry back to the tent as fast as possible for reinforcements. Ordinarily, he would have done so at once, but this time he was still smarting a bit at his poor marksmanship in the case of the "lucifee," and the sight of the track in the snow suggested the idea of winning a reputation for himself by killing a bear without any assistance from the others. It was a rash and foolish notion; but then boys will be boys.

Moving forward cautiously, he approached within ten yards of the cave and then halted again, bringing his rifle forward so as to be ready to fire at a moment's notice. Bending down until his eyes were on a level with the opening, he tried hard to peer into its depths; but the darkness was too deep to pierce, and he could not make out anything. Then he bethought him of another expedient. Picking up a lump of snow, he pressed it into a ball and threw it into the cave, at the same time shouting out, "Hallo there! Anybody inside?" A proceeding that capped the climax of his rashness and produced quite as sensational a result as he could possibly have desired, for the next moment a deep angry roar issued from the rocky retreat and a fiery pair of eyes gleamed out from its shadows. The critical moment had come, and taking aim a little below the shining orbs, so as to make sure of hitting, Frank pulled the trigger. The report of the rifle and the roar of the bear followed close upon one another, awaking the echoes of the adjoining heights. Then came a moment's silence, broken the next instant by a cry of alarm from Frank; for the bear, instead of writhing in the agonies of death, was charging down upon him with open mouth! Once more he had missed his mark and only wounded when he should have killed.

There was but one thing for him to do—to flee for his life; and uttering a shout of "Help! help!"

with all the strength of his lungs, he threw down his rifle and started for the tent at the top of his speed.

It was well for him that the snow still lay deep upon the ground, and that he was so expert in the use of his snow-shoes; for while the bear wallowed heavily in the drifts, he flew lightly over them, so that for a time the furious creature lost ground rather than gained upon him. For a hundred yards the boy and bear raced through the forest, Frank continuing his cries for help while he ran. Looking back for an instant, he saw that the bear had not yet drawn any nearer, and, terrified as he was, the thought flashed into his mind that if the brute followed him all the way to the camp he would soon be despatched by the men, and then he, Frank, would be entitled to some credit for thus bringing him to execution.

On sped the two in their race for life, the boy skimming swiftly over the soft snow, the bear ploughing his way madly through it, until more than half the distance to the camp had been accomplished. If Johnston had heard the report of the rifle and Frank's wild cries for help, he should be coming into sight now, and with intense anxiety Frank looked ahead in hopes of seeing him emerge from the trees which clustered thickly in that direction. But there was no sign of him yet; and shouting again as loudly as he could, the boy pressed strenuously forward. There was greater need for exertion than ever, for he had reached a spot where the snow was not very deep and had been firmly packed by the wind, so that the bear's broad feet sank but little in it, and his rate of speed ominously increased. So close was the fierce creature coming that Frank could hear his paws pattering on the snow and his deep panting breath.

Oh why did not Johnston appear? Surely he must have heard Frank's cries. Ah, there he was, just bursting through the trees into the opening, with Laberge and Booth close at his heels. Frank's heart bounded with joy, and he was tempted to take a glance back to see how close the bear had got. It was not a wise thing to do, and he came near paying dearly for doing it; for at the same instant his snowshoes caught in each other, and before he could recover himself he fell headlong in the snow with the bear right upon him.

CHAPTER XI.

THE GREAT SPRING DRIVE.

AT the sight of Frank's fall the three men gave a simultaneous shout of alarm that caused the bear to halt for a moment in his fierce pursuit, and lifting his head to look angrily in the direction from which the sound had come. This action saved the helpless boy—striving to regain his feet only a yard or two in front of him—from serious injury, if not from death. The instant the creature's broad breast was exposed, Johnston threw his rifle to his shoulder, and without waiting to take aim, but ejaculating a fervent "Help me, O God!" pulled the trigger. The report of the rifle rang out sharp and clear, the heavy bullet sped through the air straight to its mark, and with it embedded in his heart the mighty animal, leaving untouched the boy at his feet, made a mad bound across his body to reach the assailant who had given him his death wound.

But it was a vain though gallant attempt. Ere he was half-way to the foreman, he staggered and rolled over upon the snow, and before he could lift himself again the men were upon him, and Laberge, swinging his keen axe high in the air, brought it down with a mighty blow upon the brute's slanting forehead, letting daylight into his brain. Not even a bear could survive such a stroke, and without a struggle the creature yielded up its life.

Instantly the foreman sprang to Frank's side and lifted him upon his feet.

"My dear boy!" he cried, his face aflame with anxious love, as he clasped Frank passionately in his arms, "are you hurt at all? Did he touch you?"

What between his previous exertions and the big man's mighty embrace, poor Frank had hardly enough breath left in him to reply, but he managed to gasp out,—

"Not a bit. He never touched me."

"Are you quite sure now?" persisted Johnston, whose anxiety could not be at once relieved. "O my lad! my heart stood still when you fell down right in front of the brute."

"I'm quite sure, Mr. Johnston," said Frank. "See!" And to prove his words he gave a jump into the air, threw up his arms, and shouted, "Hip! hip! hurrah!" with the full force of his lungs.

"God be praised!" exclaimed the foreman. "What a wonderful escape! Let us kneel down right here, and give Him thanks," he added, suiting his action to his words. Frank at once followed his example; so too did Laberge and Booth; and there in the midst of the forest-wilds this strange praise-meeting was held over the body of the fierce creature from whose murderous rage Frank had been so happily delivered.

Johnston sent Laberge back to the tent for the toboggan, and before darkness set in the bear was dragged thither, where the two men skilfully skinned him by the light of the camp fire, and stretched the pelt out to dry.

The quartette had a long talk over the whole affair after supper had been disposed of. Frank was plied with questions which he took much pleasure in answering, for naturally enough he felt himself to be in some measure the hero of the occasion. While he could not help admiring and cordially praising Frank's audacity, the foreman felt bound to reprove him for it, and to impress upon him the necessity of showing more caution in future, or he might get himself into a situation of danger from which there might be no one at hand to deliver him. Frank, by this time thoroughly sobered down, listened dutifully, and readily promised to be more careful if he ever came across bear tracks again.

"Anyway, my boy," said Johnston, "you won't go home empty-handed; and when your mother sees those two skins, which are both pretty good ones, she'll think more of you than she ever did before."

"Yes, but you know," said Frank, "both skins oughtn't to be mine, for I didn't kill either of the animals."

"Neither you did, Frank," replied Johnston, "but you came mighty near killing the one, and the other came mighty near killing you; so I think it's only fair you should have both.—Don't you think so, mates?" turning to the men.

"Ah, *oui*," exclaimed Laberge, with a vigorous nod of his head.

"Of course," added Booth, no less emphatically; and so the matter was settled very much to Frank's satisfaction.

The next day the tent was packed and the little party set out for the shanty, which was reached in good time without anything eventful occurring on the way. They found the work of getting the logs down upon the ice well nigh completed, and the foreman's return giving an impetus to the men's exertions, it was finished in a few days more, and then there was nothing to do but to await the breaking up of the ice.

They were not kept long in expectancy. The sun was now in full vigour; before his burning rays the snow and ice fled in utter rout; and the frost king, confessing defeat, withdrew his grasp from the Kippewa, which, as if rejoicing in its release, went rippling and bounding merrily on toward the great river beyond, bearing upon its bosom the many thousand logs which represented the hard labour of Camp Kippewa during the long cold winter months that were now past and gone. The most arduous and exciting phase of the lumberman's life had begun, the great spring drive, as they call it, and for weeks to come he would be engaged playing the part of shepherd after a strange fashion, with huge, clumsy, unruly logs for his flock, and the rushing river for the highway along which they should be driven.

The shantymen were divided into two parties, one section taking the teams and camp-belongings back to the depot, the other and much larger section following the logs in their journey to the mills. Johnston put himself at the head of the latter, and Frank, of course, accompanied him, for the foreman was no less anxious to have him than the boy was to go. The bonds of affection that bound the two were growing stronger every day they were together. Frank regarded Johnston as the preserver of his life, and Johnston, on his part, looked upon Frank as having been in God's hands the means of bringing light and joy to his soul. It might be said, without exaggeration, that either of them would risk his life in the other's behalf with the utmost willingness.

The journey down the river had to be done in light marching order. Not much baggage could be carried, so as not to burden too heavily the three or four "*bonnes*," as they call the long, light, flat-bottomed boats peculiar to lumbermen, which had been all winter awaiting the time when their services would be required. The shore work being beyond his strength, Frank was given a place in one of the *bonnes* along with Baptiste, Laberge, and part of the commissariat, and it was their duty to precede the main body of the men, and have their dinner and supper ready for them when they came up. In this way Frank would get a perfect view of the whole business of river driving, and he was in high feather as they made a start on a beautiful morning in early May, with the sun shining brightly, the air soft and balmy, and the river reflecting the blue of the unclouded heavens.

"Now take good care of Baptiste and the grub," said Johnston, with a smile, as he pushed the boat in which Frank was sitting off into the stream. "If you let anything happen to them, Frank, I don't know what we'll do to you."

"I'll do my best, sir," replied Frank, smiling back. "The boat won't upset if I can help it, and as Baptiste can't swim, he'll do his best to be careful too; won't you, Baptiste?"

"*Vraiment, mon cher*," cried Baptiste. "If we upset—poor Baptiste! zat will be the last of him." And he shrugged his fat shoulders and made a serio-comic grimace that set everybody laughing.

If the Kippewa, through all its course, had been as deep and free from obstructions as it was opposite the lumber camp, the river drivers would have had an easy time of it getting their wooden flock to market. But none of the rivers in this part of the country go quietly on their way from source to outlet. Falls and rapids are of frequent occurrence, and it is these which add difficulty and danger to the lumberman's work. Carrying pike-poles and cant-hooks, the former being simply long tough ash poles with a sharp spike on the business end, and the latter shorter stouter poles, something like the handle of a shovel, with a curious curved iron attachment that took a firm grip of a log and enabled the worker to roll its lazy bulk over and over in the direction he desired—with these weapons taking the place of the axe and saw, the men set off on their journey down the river side, two of the boats going ahead, and two bringing up the rear.

Frank felt in great spirits. He was thoroughly expert in the management of a *bonne*, and the voyage down the river in this lovely spring weather could be only continued enjoyment, especially as beyond steering the boat he had nothing to do, and it would be practically one long holiday. There were nearly twenty thousand logs to be guided, coaxed, rolled, and shoved for one hundred miles or more through sullen pools, sleeping reaches, turbulent rapids, and roaring falls, where, as if they were living things, they would seem to exhaust every possible means of delay. The way in which they would stick at some critical point and pile one upon another, until the whole river was blocked, defies description; and one seeing the spectacle for the first time might well be pardoned if he were to be positive that there could be no way of bringing order out of so hopeless a confusion, and releasing the tangled obstructed mass.

For the first few days matters went very smoothly, the river being deep and swift, and the logs giving little trouble. Of course, numbers of them were continually stranding on the banks, but the watchful drivers soon spied them out, and with a push of the pike-pole, or drag of the cant-hook, sent them floating off again on their journey. At mid-day all the men would gather about Baptiste's kettles and dispose of a hearty dinner, and then again at night they would leave the logs to look after themselves while they ate their supper and talked, and then lay down to rest their weary bodies. But this condition of things was too good to last. In due time the difficulties began to show themselves, and then Frank saw the most exciting and dangerous phase of a lumberman's life—a part of it with which when he grew older he must himself become familiar if he would be master of the whole business, as it was his ambition to be.

THE GREAT SPRING DRIVE.

The great army of logs, forging onward slowly or swiftly, according to the force of the current, would come to a point where the stream narrowed and jagged rocks thrust their unwelcome heads above the surface. The vanguard of the army, perhaps, passing either to right or left of the rocks, would go on its way unchecked. But when the main body came up, and the whole stream was full of drifting logs, some clumsy tree trunk going down broadside first would bring up short against the rock. As quickly as a crowd will gather in a city street, the other logs would cluster about the one that obstructed their passage. There would be no stopping the on-rush. In less time than it takes to describe it, a hundred logs would be jostling one another in the current; and every minute the confusion would increase, until ere long the disordered mass would stretch from shore to shore, the whole stream would be blocked up, and the event most dreaded by the river driver would have taken place, to wit, a log jam.

The worst place that Johnston had to encounter in getting his drive of logs to the river was at the Black Rapids, and never will Frank forget the thrilling excitement of that experience. These rapids were the terror of the Kippewa lumbermen. They were situated in the swiftest part of the river, and if Nature had in cold blood tried her utmost to give the despoilers of her forest a hard nut to crack she could scarcely have succeeded better. The boiling current was divided into two portions by a jagged spur of rock that thrust itself above the surging waters, and so sure as a log came broadside against this projection it was caught and held in a firm embrace.

Johnston thoroughly understood this, and had taken every care to prevent a jam occurring; and if it had been possible for him to do what was in his mind—namely, to land upon the troublesome rock, and with his pike-pole push back again into the current every log that threatened to stick—the whole drive would have slipped safely by. He did make a gallant attempt to carry this out, putting four of the best oarsmen into Frank's boat, and trying again and again to force his way through the fierce current to the rock, while Frank watched him with breathless interest from the bank. But, strain and tug as the oarsmen might, the eddying, whirling stream was too strong for them, and swept them past the rock again and again, until at length the foreman had to give up his design as impracticable.

It was exciting work, and Frank longed very

much to be in the boat; but Johnston, indulgent as he was toward his favourite, refused him this time.

"No, no, Frank; I couldn't think of it," he said decidedly. "It's too risky a business. The *bonne* might be smashed any time, and if it did we'd run a poor chance of getting out of these rapids. More than one good man has gone to his death here."

"Have there been men killed in these rapids?" Frank asked, with a look of profound concern at his big friend, who was taking such risks. "The poor fellows! What a dreadful death! They must have been dashed against the rocks. Surely you won't try it again, will you?" For it was dinner-time, and all hands were taking a welcome rest before resuming the toils of the day.

Johnston thoroughly understood and appreciated the boy's anxiety in his behalf, and there was a look of wonderful tenderness in his eyes as he answered him:—

"I must try it once more, Frank; for if I can only get out to that rock there'll be no jam this day. But don't you worry. I've taken bigger risks and come out all right."

So he made one more attempt, while Frank watched every movement of the boat, praying earnestly for its preservation. Again he failed, and the *bonne* returned to the bank unharmed. But hardly had the weary men thrown themselves down for a brief spell of rest than what they all so dreaded happened. One of the logs, getting into a cross eddy, rolled broadside against the rock. It was caught and held fast. Another and another charged against it and stayed there. The main body of the drive was now passing down, and every moment the jam increased in size. Soon it would fill the whole stream. Yet the lumbermen were powerless to prevent its growth. They could do nothing until it had so checked the current that it would be possible to make a way over to its centre.

So soon as this took place, Johnston, accompanied by three of his best men, armed with axes and cant-hooks, leaping from log to log with the sure agility only lumbermen could show, succeeded in reaching the heart of the jam, and at once proceeded to attack it with tremendous energy. One log after another was detached from the disordered mass and sent whirling off down stream, until at the end of an hour's arduous exertion, the key-piece—that is, the log that had caused all the trouble—was found.

"Now, my boys," said Johnston to his men, "get

ashore as quick as you can. I'll stay and cut out the key-piece."

The men demurred for a moment. They were reluctant to leave their chief alone in a position of such extreme peril. But he commanded them to go.

"There's only one man wanted," he said; "and I'll do it myself. It's no use you risking your lives too."

So the men obeyed, and returned to the bank to join the group watching Johnston's movements with intense anxiety. They all knew as well as he did the exceeding peril of his position, and not one of them would breathe freely until he had accomplished his task, and found his way safely back to the shore.

CHAPTER XII.

HOME AGAIN.

FOR so large a man the foreman showed an agility that was really wonderful, as he leaped from log to log with the swiftness and sureness of a chamois. He had been lumbering all his life, and there was nothing that fell to the lumberman's experience with which he was not perfectly familiar. Yet it is doubtful if he ever had a more difficult or dangerous task than that before him now. The "key-piece" of the jam was fully exposed, and once it was cut in two it would no longer hold the accumulation of logs together. They would be released from their bondage, and springing forward with the full force of the pent-up current, would rush madly down stream, carrying everything before them.

But what would Johnston do in the midst of this tumult? A few more moments would tell; for his

HOME AGAIN. 145

axe was dealing tremendous strokes, before which the key-piece, stout though it was, must soon yield. Ah, it is almost severed. The foreman pauses for an instant and glances keenly around, evidently in order to see what will be his best course of action when the jam breaks. Frank, in an agony of apprehension and anxiety, has sunk to his knees, his lips moving in earnest prayer, while his eyes are fixed on his beloved friend. Johnston's quick glance falls upon him, and, catching the significance of his attitude, his face is irradiated with a heavenly light of love as he calls out across the boiling current,—

"God bless you, Frank! Keep praying."

Then he returns to his work. The keen axe flashes through the air in stroke after stroke. At length there comes a sound that cannot be mistaken. The foreman throws aside his axe and prepares to jump for life; and, like one man, the breathless onlookers shout together as the key-piece rends in two, and the huge jam, suddenly released, bursts away from the rock and charges tumultuously down the river.

If ever man needed the power of prompt decision, it was the foreman then. To the men on shore there seemed no possible way of escape from the avalanche of logs; and Frank shut his eyes lest he should have to witness a dreadful tragedy. A cry from the men caused him to open them again quickly, and when he looked at the rock it was untenanted— Johnston had disappeared! Speechless with dread, he turned to the man nearest him, his blanched countenance expressing the inquiry he could not utter.

"He's there," cried the man, pointing to the whirl of water behind the body of logs. "He dived."

And so it was. Recognizing that to remain in the way of the jam was to court certain death, the foreman chose the desperate alternative of diving beneath the logs, and allowing them to pass over him before he rose to the surface. Great was the relief of Frank and the others when, amid the foaming water, Johnston's head appeared, and he struck out to keep himself afloat. But it was evident that he had little strength left, and was quite unable to contend with the mighty current. Good swimmer as he was, the danger of drowning threatened him.

Frank's quick eyes noticed this, and like a flash the fearless boy, not stopping to call any of the others to his aid, bounded down the bank to where the *bonne* lay upon the shore, shoved her off into deep water, springing in over the bow as she slipped away, and in another moment was whirling down the river, crying out at the top of his voice,—

"I'm coming! I'll save you! Keep up!"

His eager shouts reached Johnston's ears, and the sight of the boat, pitching and tossing as the current swept it toward him, inspired him to renewed exertion. He struggled to get in the way of the boat, and succeeded so well that Frank, leaning over the side as far as he dared, was able to seize his outstretched hand and hold it until he could grasp the gunwale himself with a grip that no current could loosen. A glad shout of relief went up from the men at sight of this, and Frank, having made sure that the foreman was now out of danger, seized the oars and began to ply them vigorously with the purpose of beaching the *bonne* at the first opportunity. They had to go some distance before this could be done, but Johnston held on firmly, and presently a projecting point was reached, against which Frank steered the boat; and the moment she was aground, he hastened to the stern and helped the foreman ashore, the latter having just strength enough left to drag himself out of the water and fall in a limp, dripping heap upon the ground.

"God bless you, Frank dear," he said, as soon as he

recovered his breath. "You've saved my life again. I never could have got ashore if you hadn't come after me. One of the logs must have hit me on the head when I was diving, for I felt so faint and dizzy when I came up that I thought it was all over with me. But, thank God, I'm a live man still; and I'm sure it's not for nothing that I've been spared."

The men all thought it a plucky act on Frank's part to go off alone in the boat to the foreman's rescue, and showered unstinted praise upon him; all of which he took very quietly, for, indeed, he felt quite sufficiently rewarded in that his venture was crowned with success. The exciting incident of course threw everybody out in their work, and when they returned to it they found that the logs had taken advantage of their being left uncared for to play all sorts of queer pranks and run themselves aground in every conceivable fashion.

But the river drivers did not mind this very much. The hated Black Rapids were passed, and the rest of the Kippewa was comparatively smooth sailing. So, with song and joke, they toiled away until all their charges were afloat again and gliding steadily onward toward their goal. Thenceforward they had little interruption in their course; and Frank found the life wonderfully pleasant, drifting idly all day long in the *bonne*, and camping at night beside the river, the weather being bright, and warm, and delightful all the time.

So soon as the Kippewa rolled its burden of forest spoils out upon the broad bosom of the Ottawa—the Grand River, as those who live beside its banks love to call it—the work of the river drivers was over. The logs that had caused them so much trouble were now handed over to the care of a company which gathered them up into "tows," and with powerful steamers dragged them down the river until the sorting grounds were reached, where they were turned into the "booms" to await their time for execution— in other words, their sawing up.

Frank felt really sorry when the driving was over. He loved the water, and would have been glad to spend the whole summer upon it. He was telling Johnston this as they were talking together on the evening of the last day upon the Kippewa. Johnston had been saying to him how glad he must be that the work was all over, and that they now could go over to the nearest village and take the stage for home. But Frank did not entirely agree with him.

"I'm not anxious to go home by stage," said he.

"I'd a good deal rather stick to the river. I think it's just splendid, so long as the weather's fine."

"Why, what a water-dog you are, Frank!" said the foreman, laughing. "One would think you'd have had enough of the water by this time."

"Not a bit of it," said Frank, returning the smile. "The woods in winter, and the water in summer—that's what I enjoy."

"Well, but aren't you in a hurry to get home and see your mother again?" queried Johnston.

"Of course I am," answered Frank. "But, you see, a day or two won't make much difference, for she doesn't know just when to look for me; and I've never been on this part of the Ottawa, and want to see it ever so much."

"Well—let me see," reflected Johnston. "How can we manage it? You'd soon get sick of the steamers. They're mortal slow and very dirty. Besides, they don't encourage passengers, or they'd have too many of them. But hold on!" he exclaimed, his face lighting up with a new idea. "I've got it. How would you like to finish the rest of the trip home on a square timber raft? There'll be one passing any day, and I know 'most all the men in the business, so there'll be no difficulty about getting a passage."

"The very idea!" cried Frank, jumping up and bringing his hand down upon his thigh with a resounding slap. "Nothing would please me better. Oh, what fun it will be shooting the slides!" And he danced about in delight at the prospect.

"All right then, my lad," said Johnston, smiling at the boy's exuberance. "We'll just wait here until a raft comes along, and then we'll board her and ask the fellows to let us go down with them. They won't refuse."

They had not long to wait, for the very next day a huge raft hove in sight—a real floating island of mighty timbers—and on going out to it in the *bonne*, Johnston was glad to find that the foreman in charge was an old friend who would be heartily pleased at having his company for the rest of the voyage. So he and Frank brought their scanty baggage on board, and joined themselves to the crew of men that, with the aid of a towing steamer, were navigating this very strange kind of craft down the river.

This was an altogether novel experience for Frank, and he found it much to his liking. The raft was an immense one.

"As fine a lot of square timber as I ever took down," said its captain proudly. "It's worth five thousand pounds if it's worth a penny."

Five thousand pounds! Frank's eyes opened wide at the mention of this vast sum, and he wondered to himself if he should ever be the owner of such a valuable piece of property. Although he had begun as a chore-boy, his ambition was by no means limited to his becoming in due time a foreman like Johnston, or even an overseer like Alec Stewart. He allowed his imagination to carry him forward to a day of still greater things, when he should be his own master, and have foremen and overseers under him. This slow sailing down the river was very favourable to day dreaming, and Frank could indulge himself to his heart's content during the long lovely spring days. There were more than twoscore men upon the raft, the majority of them habitants and half-breeds, and they were as full of songs as robins; especially in the evening after supper, when they would gather about the great fire always burning on its clay bed in the centre of the raft, and with solo and chorus awake the echoes of the placid river.

In common with the rivers which pour into it, the Ottawa is broken by many falls and rapids, and to have attempted to run the huge raft over one of these would have insured its complete destruction. But this difficulty is duly provided for. At one side of the fall a "slide" is built—that is, a contrivance something like a canal, with sides and bottom of heavy timber, and having a steep slope down which the water rushes in frantic haste to the level below. Now the raft is not put together in one piece, but is made up of a number of "cribs"—a crib being a small raft containing fifteen to twenty timbers, and being about twenty-four feet wide by thirty feet in length. At the head of the slide the big raft is separated into the cribs, and these cribs make the descent one at a time, each having three or four men on board.

Shooting the slides, as it is called, is a most delightful amusement to people whose nerves don't bother them. Frank had heard so much about it that he was looking forward to it from the time he boarded the raft, and now at Des Joachim Falls he was to have the realization. He went down in one of the first cribs, and this is the way he described the experience to his mother:—

"But, mother, the best fun of the whole thing is shooting the slides. I just wish there was a slide near Calumet, so that I could take you down and let you see how splendid it is. Why, it's just like—let me see—I've got it! It's just like tobogganing on water. You jump on board the crib at the mouth of the slide, you know, and it moves along very slowly at first, until it gets to the edge of the first slant; then it takes a sudden start, and away it goes shooting down like greased lightning, making the water fly up all around you, just like the snow does when you're tobogganing. Oh, but if it isn't grand! The timbers of the crib rub against the bottom of the slide, and groan and creak as if it hurt them. And then, besides coming in over the bow, the water spurts up between the timbers, so that you have to look spry or you're bound to get soaking wet. I got drenched nearly every time; but that didn't matter, for the sun soon made me dry again, and it was too good fun to mind a little wetting."

Frank felt quite sorry when the last of the slides was passed, and wished there were twice as many on the route of the raft. But presently he had something else to occupy his thoughts, for each day brought him nearer to Calumet, and soon his journeyings by land and water would be ended, and he would be at home again to make his mother's heart glad.

It was the perfection of a spring day when the raft, moving in its leisurely fashion—for was not the whole summer before it?—reached Calumet, and Mrs.

Kingston, sitting alone in her cottage, and wondering when her boy would make his appearance, was surprised by an unceremonious opening of the front door, a quick step in the hall, and a sudden enfolding by two stout arms, while a voice that she had not heard for months shouted in joyous accents,—

"Here I am, mother darling, safe and sound, right side up with care, and oh, so glad to be at home again!"

Mrs. Kingston returned the fond embrace with interest, and then held Frank off at arm's-length to see how much he had changed during his six months' absence. She found him both taller and stouter, and with his face well browned by the exposure to the bright spring sunshine.

"You went away a boy, and you've come back almost a man, Frank," she said, her eyes brimming with tears of joy. "But you're my own boy the same as ever; aren't you, darling?"

It was many a day before Frank reached the end of his story of life at the lumber camp, for Mrs. Kingston never wearied of hearing all about it. When she learned of his different escapes from danger, the inclination of her heart was to beseech him to be content with one winter in the woods, and to take up some other occupation. But she wisely said nothing, for there could be no doubt as to the direction in which Frank's heart inclined, and she determined not to interfere.

When in the following autumn Frank went back to the forest, he was again under Johnston's command, but not as chore-boy. He was appointed clerk and checker, with liberty to do as much chopping or other work as he pleased. Whatever his duty was he did it with all his might, doing it heartily as to the Lord and not unto men, so that he found increasing favour in his employer's eyes, rising steadily higher and higher until, while still a young man, he was admitted into partnership, and had the sweet satisfaction of realizing the day dreams of that first trip down the Ottawa on a timber raft.

Yet he never forgot what he had learned when chore-boy of Camp Kippewa, and out of that experience grew a practical philanthropic interest in the well-being and advancement of his employés, that made him the most popular and respected "lumber-king" on the river.

THE END.

Our Boys' Select Library.

Stories of Adventure, Travel, and Discovery.

Post 8vo, cloth extra, uniform binding. Price 2s. 6d. each.

Beyond the Himalayas. A Book for Boys. By JOHN GEDDIE, F.R.G.S., Author of "The Lake Regions of Central Africa," etc. With 9 Engravings.

The Castaways. A Story of Adventure in the Wilds of Borneo. By Captain MAYNE REID.

Frank Redcliffe. A Story of Travel and Adventure in the Forests of Venezuela. A Book for Boys. By ACHILLES DAUNT, Author of "The Three Trappers," etc. With numerous Illustrations.

In the Land of the Moose, the Bear, and the Beaver. Adventures in the Forests of the Athabasca. By ACHILLES DAUNT, Author of "The Three Trappers." With Illustrations.

In the Bush and on the Trail. Adventures in the Forests of North America. A Book for Boys. By M. BENEDICT REVOIL. With 70 Illustrations.

The Lake Regions of Central Africa. A Record of Modern Discovery. By JOHN GEDDIE, F.R.G.S. With 32 Illustrations.

Lost in the Backwoods. A Tale of the Canadian Forest. By Mrs. TRAILL, Author of "In the Forest," etc. With 32 Engravings.

The Meadows Family; or, Fireside Stories of Adventure and Enterprise. By M. A. PAULL, Author of "Tim's Troubles," etc. With Illustrations.

The Three Trappers. A Book for Boys. By ACHILLES DAUNT, Author of "In the Land of the Moose, the Bear, and the Beaver." With 11 Engravings.

Wrecked on a Reef; or, Twenty Months in the Auckland Isles. A True Story of Shipwreck, Adventure, and Suffering. With 40 Illustrations.

Ralph's Year in Russia. A Story of Travel and Adventure in Eastern Europe. By ROBERT RICHARDSON, Author of "Almost a Hero," etc. With 8 Engravings.

Scenes with the Hunter and the Trapper in Many Lands. Stories of Adventures with Wild Animals. With Engravings.

The Forest, the Jungle, and the Prairie; or, Tales of Adventure and Enterprise in Pursuit of Wild Animals. With numerous Engravings.

The Island Home; or, The Young Castaways. A Story of Adventure in the Southern Seas. With Illustrations.

T. NELSON AND SONS, LONDON, EDINBURGH, AND NEW YORK.

Travel and Adventure.

Jack Hooper. His Adventures at Sea and in South Africa. By VERNEY LOVETT CAMERON, C.B., D.C.L., Commander Royal Navy; Author of "Across Africa," etc. With 23 Full-page Illustrations. Price 4s., or with gilt edges, 5s.

"*Our author has the immense advantage over many writers of boys' stories that he describes what he has seen, and does not merely draw on his imagination and on books.*"—SCOTSMAN.

With Pack and Rifle in the Far South-West. Adventures in New Mexico, Arizona, and Central America. By ACHILLES DAUNT, Author of "Frank Redcliffe," etc. With 30 Illustrations. 4s., or with gilt edges, 5s.

A delightful book of travel and adventure, with much valuable information as to the geography and natural history of the wild American "Far West."

In Savage Africa; or, The Adventures of Frank Baldwin from the Gold Coast to Zanzibar. By VERNEY LOVETT CAMERON, C.B., D.C.L., Commander Royal Navy; Author of "Jack Hooper," etc. With 32 Illustrations. Crown 8vo, cloth extra, gilt edges. Price 4s., or with gilt edges, 5s.

Early English Voyagers; or, The Adventures and Discoveries of Drake, Cavendish, and Dampier. Numerous Illustrations. Price 4s., or with gilt edges, 5s.

The title of this work describes the contents. It is a handsome volume, which will be a valuable gift for young persons generally, and boys in particular. There are included many interesting illustrations and portraits of the three great voyagers.

Sandford and Merton. A Book for the Young. By THOMAS DAY. Illustrated. Post 8vo, cloth extra. Price 2s. 6d.

Our Sea-Coast Heroes; or, Tales of Wreck and of Rescue by the Lifeboat and Rocket. By ACHILLES DAUNT, Author of "Frank Redcliffe," etc. With numerous Illustrations. Price 2s. 6d.

Robinson Crusoe. The Life and Strange Adventures of Robinson Crusoe, of York, Mariner. Written by Himself. *Carefully Reprinted from the Original Edition.* With Memoir of De Foe, a Memoir of Alexander Selkirk, and other interesting additions. Illustrated with upwards of Seventy Engravings by KEELEY HALSWELLE. Crown 8vo, cloth ex. 3s.

An edition that every boy would be pleased to include in his library. It is handsomely bound, and the numerous illustrations assist greatly in the realization of this famous story.

The Swiss Family Robinson; or, Adventures of a Father and his Four Sons on a Desolate Island. Unabridged Translation. With 300 Illustrations. Price 3s.

A capital edition of this well-known work. As the title suggests, its character is somewhat similar to that of the famous "Robinson Crusoe." It combines, in a high degree, the two desirable qualities in a book,—instruction and amusement.

Gulliver's Travels into Several Remote Regions of the World. With Introduction and Explanatory Notes by the late Mr. ROBERT MACKENZIE, Author of "The 19th Century," "America," etc. With 20 Illustrations. Post 8vo, cloth extra. Price 3s.

"*A very handsome edition, under the editorship of Mr. Robert Mackenzie, who has supplied for it a well-written introduction and explanatory notes.... We have also here the curious original maps and a number of modern illustrations of much merit. Altogether this is a most attractive re-appearance of a famous book.*"—GLASGOW HERALD.

T. NELSON AND SONS, LONDON, EDINBURGH, AND NEW YORK.

Good Purpose Tales and Stories.

What shall I be? or, A Boy's Aim in Life. With Frontispiece and Vignette. Post 8vo, cloth extra. Price 2s.

A tale for the young. The good results of good home example and training appearing in the end, after discipline and failings.

At the Black Rocks. A Story for Boys. By the Rev. EDWARD A. RAND, Author of "Margie at the Harbour Light," etc. Post 8vo, cloth extra. Price 2s.

A story the leading characters of which are two youths. One is always full of great schemes, which invariably end in smoke, and often bring their author into trouble and humiliation; while the other, a simple, unassuming lad, says little, but always does exactly what is needed, and earns general respect and confidence.

The Phantom Picture. By the Hon. Mrs. GREENE, Author of "The Grey House on the Hill," "On Angels' Wings," etc. With Illustrations. Post 8vo, cloth extra. Price 2s.

A story of two brothers and the misery brought upon both by one of them disobeying a command of their father. The innocent boy is for a while suspected and made unhappy in consequence; but at last truth prevails and all ends well.

Archie Digby; or, An Eton Boy's Holidays. By G. E. W., Author of "Harry Bertram and his Eighth Birthday." Post 8vo, cl. ex. 2s.

A very interesting tale for boys. The hero, a clever, thoughtless young Etonian, learns during a Christmas holiday time, by humbling experience, lessons full of value for all after life.

Rhoda's Reform; or, "Owe no Man Anything." By M. A. PAULL, Author of "Tim's Troubles," "The Children's Tour," etc. Post 8vo, cloth extra. Price 2s.

Martin's Inheritance; or, The Story of a Life's Chances. A Temperance Tale. By E. VAN SOMMER, Author of "Lionel Franklin's Victory," "By Uphill Paths," etc. Post 8vo, cloth extra. Price 2s.

True Riches; or, Wealth Without Wings. By T. S. ARTHUR. Illustrated. Post 8vo, cloth extra. Price 2s.

Teaches lessons such as cannot be learned too early by those who are engaged in the active and all-absorbing duties of life.

Culm Rock; or, Ready Work for Willing Hands. A Book for Boys. By J. W. BRADLEY. Foolscap 8vo. With Engravings. 2s.

It narrates the experiences and adventures of a boy compelled by circumstances to a hard life on a stern and stormy coast.

After Years. A Story of Trials and Triumphs. By the Author of, and forming a Sequel to, "Culm Rock." With Illustrations. Foolscap 8vo, cloth extra. Price 2s.

An American tale, the sequel to "Culm Rock," showing how well Noll Trafford, in after years, fulfilled the fair promise of his early boyhood.

Conquest and Self-Conquest; or, Which Makes the Hero? Foolscap 8vo. Price 2s.

A tale very suitable for a lad under fifteen. It teaches the important lesson that the greatest of victories is the victory gained over self.

Home Principles in Boyhood. Foolscap 8vo, cloth extra. 2s.

The story of a lad who, in spite of apparent self-interest to the contrary, held firmly to the principles in which he had been instructed by Christian parents.

Illustrated Books for the Young.

The Children's Tour; or, Everyday Sights in a Sunny Land. By M. A. PAULL, Author of "Tim's Troubles," "The Meadows Family." With numerous Illustrations. Small 4to, cloth extra, gilt edges. Price 5s.

A book for children, describing scenery and adventures during a tour in Italy, taken by a family party,—the health of the eldest girl requiring a winter in the south. Much useful information is pleasantly given for young readers.

The Sea and its Wonders. By MARY and ELIZABETH KIRBY. With 174 Illustrations. Small 4to, cloth extra, gilt edges. Price 5s. Cheaper Edition, 3s. 6d.

A book for the young, not strictly scientific, but giving in a conversational style much varied information regarding the sea, its plants and living inhabitants, with all sorts of illustrative engravings.

The World at Home. Pictures and Scenes from Far-off Lands. By M. and E. KIRBY. With 100 Engravings. Small 4to, cloth extra, gilt edges. Price 5s. Cheaper Edition, 3s. 6d.

A book for the young, containing, in a number of short conversational sections, a great variety of geographical information, facts of natural history, and personal adventure; intended to bring the world, so full of wonders, to our own firesides. The whole is profusely illustrated.

Bible Stories Simply Told. By M. E. CLEMENTS, Author of "The Story of the Beacon Fire," etc. Small 4to, cloth extra, gilt edges. With numerous Illustrations. 5s. Cheaper Edition, 3s. 6d.

In this elegant volume we have stories from the Old Testament told in simple language for young people. It is divided into three sections:—I. About the Old World. II. The Patriarchs. III. The Rescue from Egypt.

Natural History for Young Folks. By Mrs. C. C. CAMPBELL. With 56 Illustrations by GIACOMELLI. In elegant binding. Post 8vo, cloth extra, gold and colours. Price 3s. 6d.

"*Evidently the result of years of research on the part of the author, Mrs. C. C. Campbell. Her object has been to simplify the more scientific side of the subject, and 'to explain how the different orders of animals, from man, the highest, down to the duck-billed platypus, resemble one another.' The book is thoroughly entertaining.*"—SATURDAY REVIEW.

Pets and Playfellows; or, Stories about Cats and Dogs. By Mrs. SURR. With Twenty-four Illustrations. Small 4to, cloth extra. Price 3s. 6d.

A rich store of interest and amusement for young people, who will find their knowledge and love of animals increased by its perusal.

The Stories of the Trees. Talks with the Children. By Mrs. W. H. DYSON, Author of "Children's Flowers," "Apples and Oranges," etc. With Illustrations. Post 8vo, cloth extra. Price 3s. 6d.

"*Well suited, by its pleasant, chatty style, to interest young people.*"—SATURDAY REVIEW.

Royal Portrait Gallery. With numerous Illustrations. Small 4to, cloth extra. Price 3s. 6d.

In this volume our kings and queens are described with pen and pencil in a way that is sure to delight and instruct young readers.

Pictures and Stories from English History. With numerous Illustrations. Small 4to, cloth extra. Price 3s. 6d.

The stories are told in a lively and attractive style, and cannot fail to create in the young a liking for the study of history.

T. NELSON AND SONS, LONDON, EDINBURGH, AND NEW YORK.

www.ingramcontent.com/pod-product-compliance
Lightning Source LLC
Chambersburg PA
CBHW030318170426
43202CB00009B/1057